The Human Body

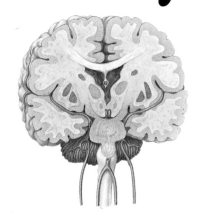

WELDON OWEN PTY LTD

Chairman: John Owen
Publisher: Sheena Coupe
Associate Publisher: Lynn Humphries
Managing Editor: Helen Bateman
Design Concept: Sue Rawkins
Senior Designer: Kylie Mulquin
Production Manager: Caroline Webber
Production Assistant: Kylie Lawson

Text: Robert Coupe
Consultant: Marie Rose, Medical Practitioner
U.S. Editors: Laura Cavaluzzo and Rebecca McEwen

04 03 02 01 00 99
10 9 8 7 6 5 4 3 2 1

Published in the United States by
Shortland Publications, Inc.
P.O. Box 6195
Denver, CO 80206-0195

Printed in Australia.
ISBN: 0-7699-0476-9

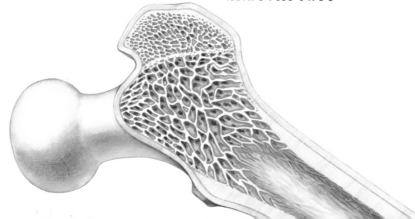

CONTENTS

IN ANCIENT TIMES

Today, doctors understand how our bodies work. If you get sick, a doctor will probably know how to cure you. In ancient Greece, more than 2,000 years ago, doctors did not understand the human body as well as we do now. When people got ill, doctors often thought that making them bleed would cure them.

DID YOU KNOW?

Doctors in ancient Greece often used herbs to cure sickness. Some thistle plants were believed to cure stomachaches and scorpion bites.

In ancient China, more than 1,000 years ago, doctors were important people. They had learned how to cure some illnesses and prevent pain. One way was to place needles under the skin in special areas of the body. Still used today, this treatment is called acupuncture.

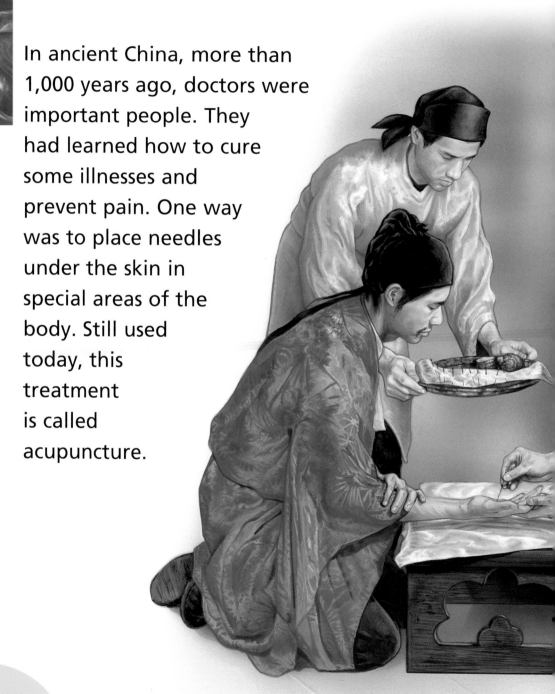

DID YOU KNOW?

The Chinese, like the Greeks, ate herbs to cure illness. Star anise, shown here, was part of many medicines.

SKIN AND NAILS

Most of the outside of your body is covered with skin. Your skin lets you feel things that you touch. It also protects you from dirt and germs and other things that could harm you, such as being bumped. Parts of your skin are covered with hair and nails.

SKIN AND COLOR

If your skin is dark, it has a lot of a substance called melanin (shown as brown spots below) in it. People with pale skin do not have very much melanin in their skin.

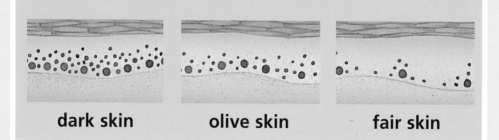

dark skin   olive skin   fair skin

AMAZING!

The patterns of skin on your fingertips are your fingerprints. Your fingerprints are not like anyone else's.

Growing Nails

Your nails grow out of roots in your skin near the ends of your fingers and toes. Nails, like hair, are not alive. That's why it doesn't hurt to cut them.

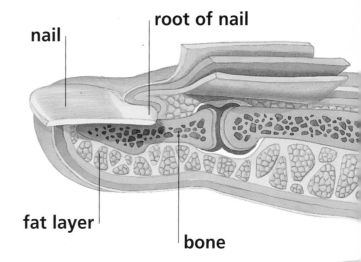

nail

root of nail

fat layer

bone

Nervous Energy

Your brain controls most of what happens in the rest of your body. It sends out messages and gets them back along millions of thin lines, called nerves. These lines travel down along your spinal cord. They branch out along the way to reach all parts of your body. The picture shows how this system works.

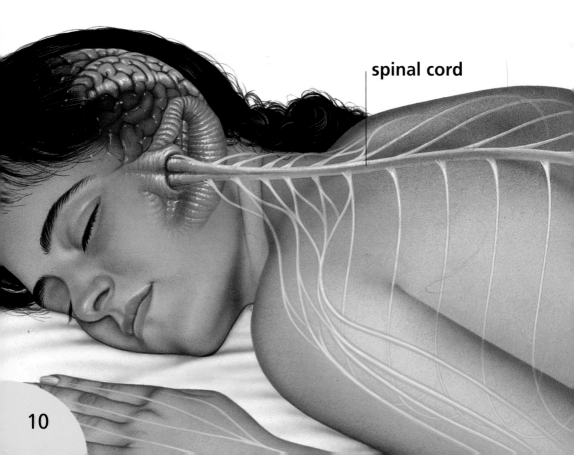

spinal cord

REFLEX ACTIONS

If you tap someone on the knee, their leg kicks up. If you touch something that is too hot, your hand pulls away. These are "reflex actions." The hand and leg do what the nerves tell them.

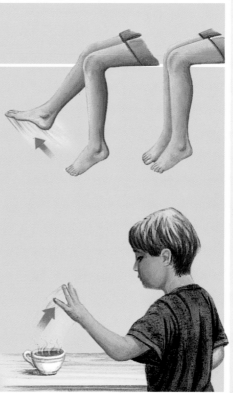

MUSCLE POWER

Under your skin and deep inside your body are hundreds of muscles. There are three kinds. You need skeletal muscle to move any part of your body. Smooth muscle helps you digest your food, and cardiac muscle is what makes your heart work.

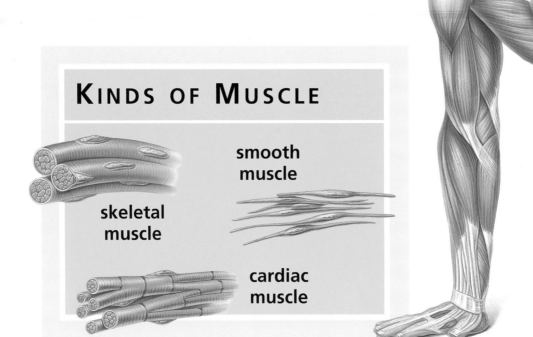

KINDS OF MUSCLE

skeletal muscle

smooth muscle

cardiac muscle

WORKING TOGETHER

Biceps and triceps are the names of two types of skeletal muscles in your arm. They work together to let you bend and straighten your arm.

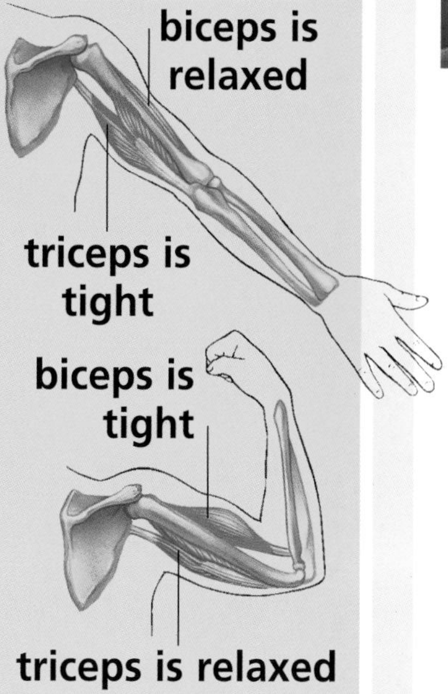

biceps is relaxed

triceps is tight

biceps is tight

triceps is relaxed

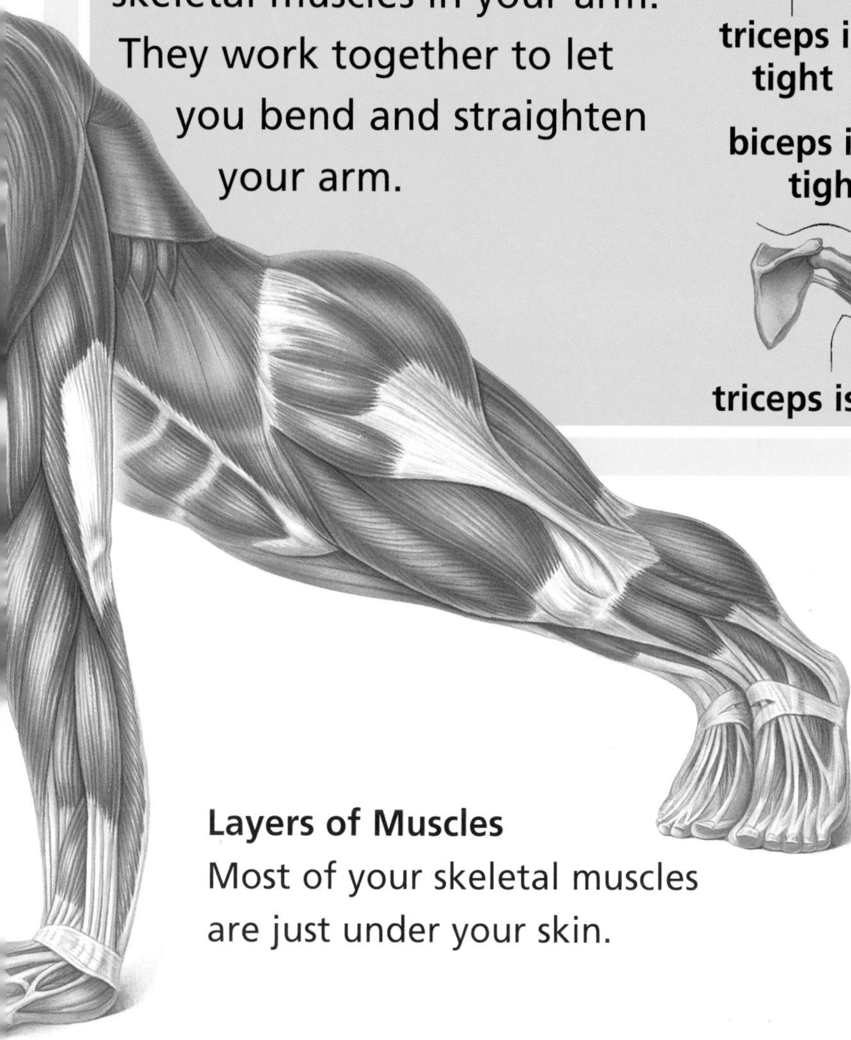

Layers of Muscles
Most of your skeletal muscles are just under your skin.

13

Skull Shapes
The domes on buildings are shaped like our skulls. This shape is strong, but light.

Florence cathedral   **human skull**

LOOKING AT BONES

Bones are like the framework of a building. They are strong and they hold your body together. Your bones are all different shapes and sizes. About half of them are the small bones in your wrists, hands, ankles, and feet. Bones have blood vessels and nerves in them. That is why it hurts when something hits one of your bones. Though they are hard, bones can bend. This helps to stop them from breaking when you fall.

bone marrow ————

AMAZING!

Your backbone, or spine, contains 24 separate bones, called vertebrae. In between these vertebrae are pieces of cartilage, which can stretch like elastic.

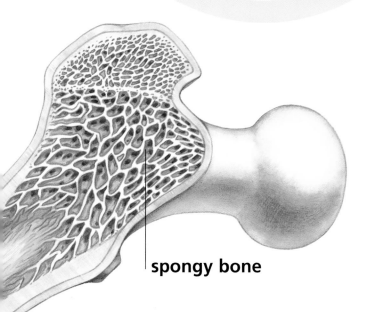

spongy bone

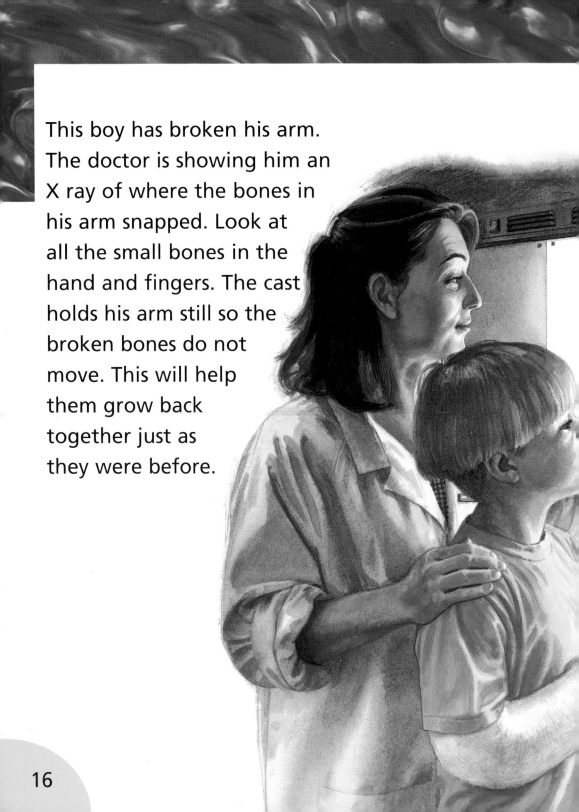

This boy has broken his arm. The doctor is showing him an X ray of where the bones in his arm snapped. Look at all the small bones in the hand and fingers. The cast holds his arm still so the broken bones do not move. This will help them grow back together just as they were before.

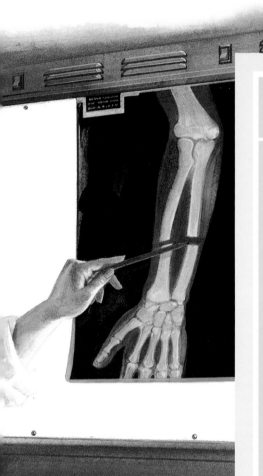

MENDING BONES

A bone bleeds when it breaks. The blood vessels and the bone slowly join up again as the bone mends.

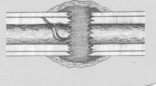

broken bone

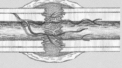

mending bone

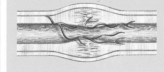

mended bone

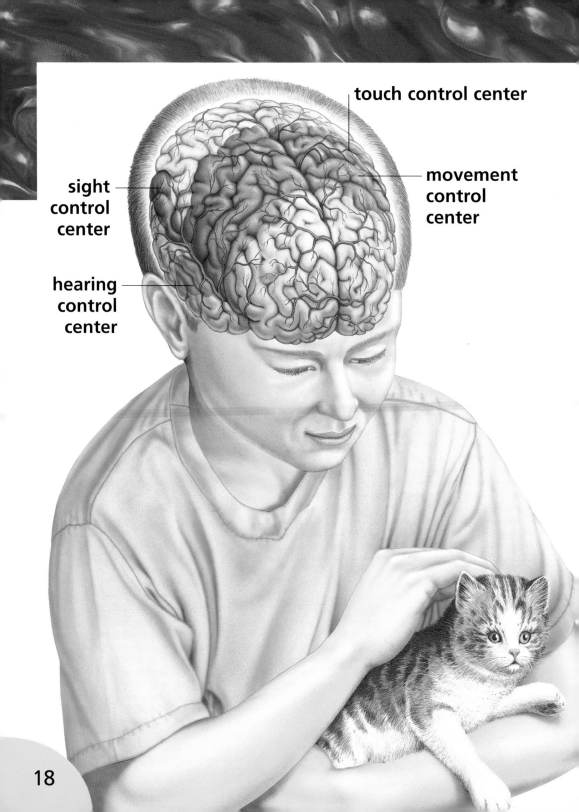

touch control center

sight control center

movement control center

hearing control center

18

THE BRAIN

Inside your head, and protected by your skull bone, is your brain. Whether you are asleep or awake, it never stops working. It controls everything that happens in your body. Through the nerves that stretch out from it, it allows you to think, feel, hear, see, taste, move, speak, and breathe. It also tells you when you need to eat or drink, or go to sleep.

PARTS OF THE BRAIN

Your brain has two main sides—the left and the right hemispheres. They are joined by a "bridge" of nerve fibers.

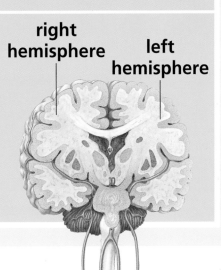

right hemisphere

left hemisphere

How We Talk

When you talk, you use your voice. In your throat you have two vocal cords. They are in your voice box, or larynx. When air comes up your windpipe, or trachea, these cords vibrate like violin strings. This makes a sound. By moving your mouth you change this sound.

Face Sounds

Look in a mirror to see how you move your tongue, lips, teeth, and cheeks to make different types of sounds.

aaah eeee oooh mmm

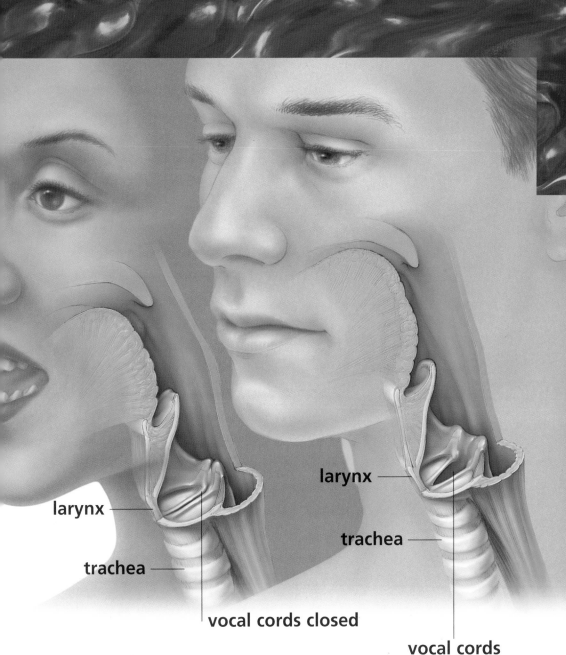

larynx

trachea

vocal cords closed

larynx

trachea

**vocal cords
open**

Open or Closed?

When you make voice sounds, your
vocal cords close up. When you are
just breathing, they stay open.

21

INSIDE THE EYE

When you look at an object, light coming from
or bouncing off of it enters your eye through the
cornea. It then goes through a hole, called a pupil.
A muscle, the iris, can make the pupil bigger or
smaller. A lens focuses a clear image on the retina,
at the back of the eye. The image then travels to
the brain along the optic nerve.

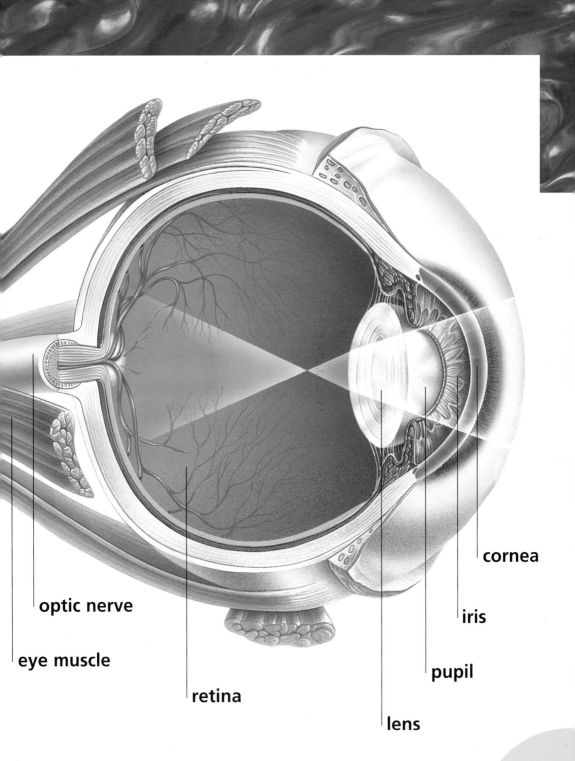

optic nerve

eye muscle

retina

lens

pupil

iris

cornea

Eyelids have several important jobs to do. You can close them to protect your eyes from bright sunlight or from wind or dust, or to block out any light when you sleep. They also keep your eyes clean. Every time you blink, the eyelid spreads a little bit of water over your eye. This comes from the tear gland under the eyelid. It washes away dust and germs.

TRY THIS!

Sometimes your eyes can trick you. Look quickly at this picture and you will see 15 squares. Stare closely at it. Can you see dots?

ONE EYE OR TWO?

Roll up a sheet of paper and copy what the boy is doing. First close your left eye. What do you see? Now open your left eye as well. What do you see now?

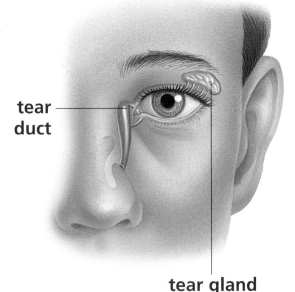

tear duct

tear gland

Tears and Crying

When you cry, tears flow into your eyes from the tear glands. Some of the tears go down the tear duct into your nose. They make your nose sniffly.

25

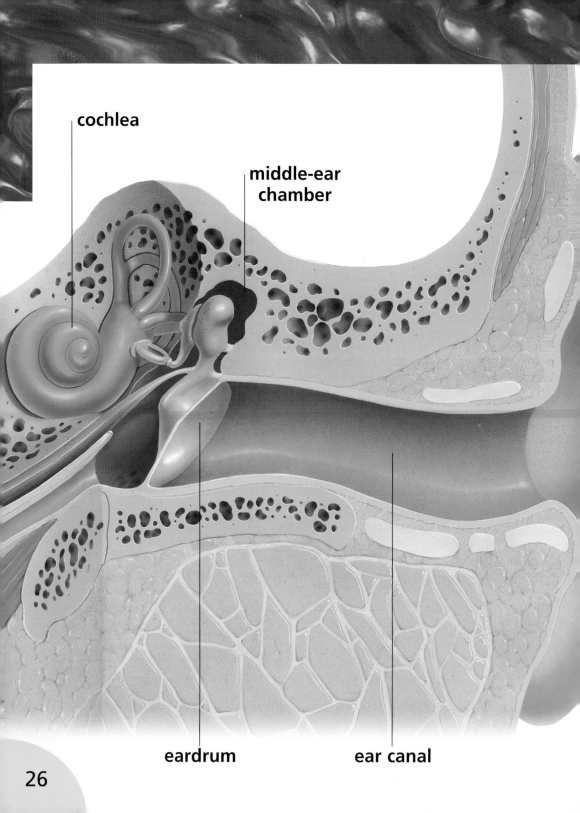

cochlea

middle-ear
chamber

eardrum

ear canal

LISTENING IN

The air around you is full of sounds. They move on air waves, which enter your ear and travel down your ear canal. They hit against a tight piece of skin called the eardrum and make it vibrate. The vibrations move into the cochlea, which is filled with fluid. This fluid moves and sends nerve signals to the brain.

DID YOU KNOW?

Your ear canal is quite long. It goes into your head as far as the corner of your eye.

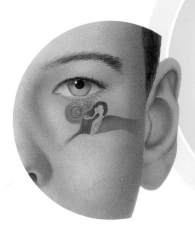

TASTE AND SMELL

When you eat, both your tongue and your nose help you enjoy your food. Saliva in your mouth mixes the flavors together, and taste buds on your tongue let you taste them. Smells float in the air and into your nose. Nerves sense these smells and send them to your brain.

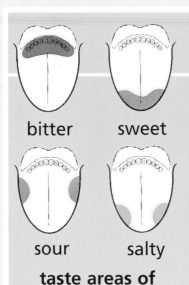

bitter   sweet

sour   salty

taste areas of the tongue

STRANGE BUT TRUE

You know the tastes of many things, but there are only four flavors—bitter, sweet, sour, and salty. These combine to make all the tastes you know.

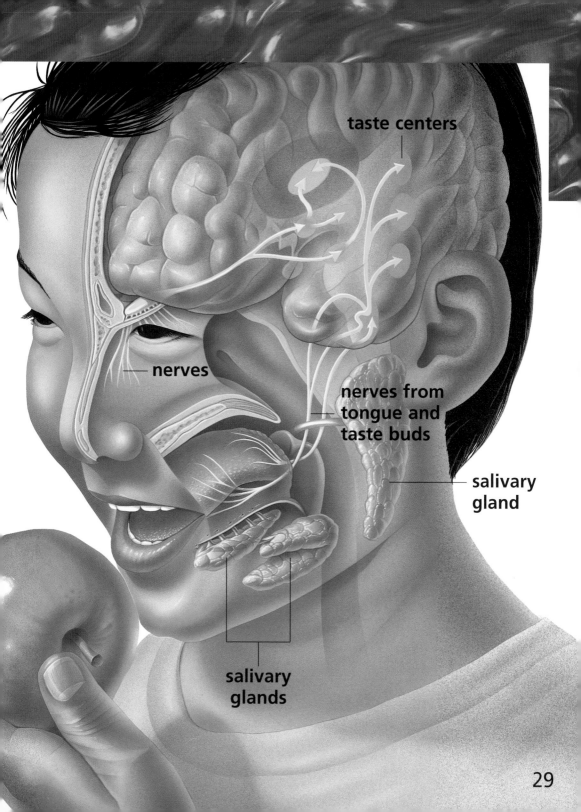

taste centers

nerves

nerves from
tongue and
taste buds

salivary
gland

salivary
glands

GLOSSARY

cartilage Firm parts of the body under the skin. Cartilage covers the joints where bones meet.

cornea The clear part at the front of the eye. Light comes into the eye through the cornea.

gland An organ that makes substances that the body needs.

saliva The spit in a person's mouth. It helps to make food soft and chewy.

spinal cord A thick stringlike cord that goes right down the back. It carries nerves from the brain.

INDEX

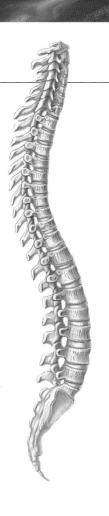

CREDITS AND NOTES

Picture and Illustration Credits
[t=top, b=bottom, l=left, r=right, c=center, F=front, B=back, C=cover, bg=background]
Susanna Addario 8bc, 9br, 14tl, 14tc, FCtr. **Ad-Libitum/ Michal Kanewski** 3tr, 22lc, 25tr, 30b. **Corel Corporation** 4–32 borders, Cbg. **John Foerster/Foerster Illustration** 21c. **Mary Foley** 20bc. **Janet Jones** 2b, 14–15bc, 16–17c, 17rc. **R. Spencer Phippen** 26c, 27bl, 11cr. **Trevor Ruth** 10–11bc, 11tr, BC. **Christine Shafner** 13tr. **Kate Sweeney/K.E. Sweeney Illustration** 12–13c, 12bl, 15tr, 22–23cr, 25bl, 29c, 28bl, 31t, FCc, FClc. **Sharif Tarabay/illustration** 3br, 4cr, 5c, 6–7c, 7rc. **Weldon Owen** 9tc. **Steve Weston/Linden Artists** 1c, 18c, 19br.

Acknowledgements
Weldon Owen would like to thank the following people for their assistance in the production of this book: Jocelyne Best, Peta Gorman, Tracey Jackson, Andrew Kelly, Sarah Mattern, Emily Wood.

⊓⊔⊓⊔⊓⊔⊓⊔⊓⊔⊓

Suddenly, *BAM!* The door slammed shut.

Atalanta ran to it. "Hey, what are you doing?"

"Making sure you stay put!" The king grinned through the small barred window in the door.

Poor Atalanta! I could tell her head was spinning. Her father had tricked her. She was definitely having a bad *heir* day.

I wanted to rip that door off of its hinges! I wanted to take Atalanta far, far away from that father of hers. But there's a whole section in *The Godly Handbook for Helping Mortals* about gods interfering between parents and their children. It's a big no-no.

"Now," said the king, puffing smoke into the room. "It's time we found you a husband."

"No!" Atalanta cried. "I am a Daughter of Artemis. I have taken a vow never to marry."

"So what?" said the king. "I have lawyers here who can get me out of any promise I make. Nothing to it. I'll put them on the case."

"No!" cried Atalanta. "I have no wish to marry!"

"Of course you do!" said the king.

A low rumble started in Atalanta's throat. She curled her upper lip in a snarl.

1 Greek Peak
2 Heroes
3 Palace of King Oeneus and
   Queen Althea
4 Palace of King Iasus and
   His Stadium
5 Persephone's Vegetable Garden
6 Honey's Cave

Go for the GOLD, ATALANTA!

By
Kate McMullan

Illustrated by
David LaFleur

VOLO
HYPERION
New York

For Joan & Doug and Naomi & Dennis
and for all the good times at Heroes

⌐⌐⌐⌐⌐⌐⌐

Many thanks to Liza Baker, Catherine Daly, Lisa
Holton, Angus Killick, Tara Lewis, Maria Padilla,
Christopher Caines, David Cashion, Monica
Mayper, and all the other maniacs at Hyperion.

Text copyright © 2003 by Kate McMullan
Illustrations copyright © 2003 by David LaFleur
Volo® is a registered trademark of Disney Enterprises, Inc. The Volo colophon is a
trademark of Disney Enterprises, Inc.

Printed in the United States of America
First Edition
1 3 5 7 9 10 8 6 4 2

ISBN 0-7868-1671-6

Library of Congress Cataloging-in-Publication Data on file.

Visit www.volobooks.com

Prologue

Greetings, mortals! It's your godly pal, Hades, Ruler of the Underworld, back again, and you know why. To tell you the truth! To right centuries of wrongs! To set things straight on the pack of lies my little brother Zeus, Ruler of the Universe and tireless myth-o-maniac (old Greek-speak for "big fat liar"), has tried to pass off as the Greek myths.

Why are the myths so messed up, you ask? Because long, long ago, Zeus got his mitts on a copy of *The Big Fat Book of Greek Myths*. As the title says, it's a big, fat book. Zeus was too lazy to read it himself, so he made his nymphs take turns reading it aloud to him. Every time a nymph got to a part Zeus didn't like, he'd yell, "FIX IT!" Then the nymphs had to scratch out that part of the story, put their heads together, and make up something that would please Zeus. If the old myth-o-maniac approved of their new version of the myth, he ordered them to write it down in the book. And the rest, as they say, is history. Make that HISstory. Zeus's story, to be exact. You can open *The Big Fat Book of Greek Myths* to any page at all and read lies, lies, nothing but lies.

Why Zeus yelled "FIX IT!" so many times when the nymphs read him the myth about the mortal Atalanta is anyone's guess. Zeus didn't have anything to do with that myth. Not until his little walk-on part right at the end. Maybe Hera, Zeus's wife and the goddess of marriage, was mad at him, and he was trying to get on her good side by giving marriage a boost. Who knows? All I know is that the myth you think you know is bull-hooey. Read it yourself right from the *Big Fat Book*. Go on, check it out:

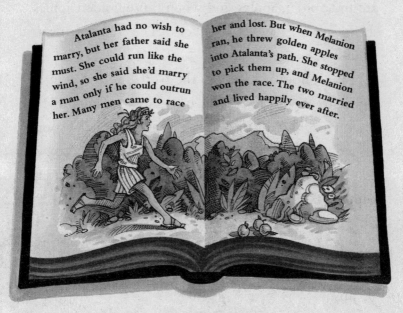

Atalanta had no wish to marry, but her father said she must. She could run like the wind, so she said she'd marry a man only if he could outrun her. Many men came to race her and lost. But when Melanion ran, he threw golden apples into Atalanta's path. She stopped to pick them up, and Melanion won the race. The two married and lived happily ever after.

It's the last part that really gets to me: "The two married and lived happily ever after." Not! The Atalanta myth is no fairy tale. It's the story of a baby girl who was abandoned by her dad, a mean, scheming, money-hungry king, because she wasn't a baby boy. But this baby girl grew up to be as big and strong as any big, strong man in Greece. She became famous, and then, of course, her dad had second thoughts and tried to get her back. At about that time, Melanion showed up and started tossing around golden apples, and when those golden apples show up in a myth, look out! They *always* mean trouble.

How about if I tell you the truth about Atalanta, right from the start? The beginning of this myth is downright embarrassing to me. I'd just as soon forget about it. But if I'm going to tell this story, and it looks like I am, then I'll tell it just the way it happened.

Chapter 1

BEARY BAD DAY

The day I first laid my godly eyes on Atalanta started out fine. My queen, Persephone, and I were sitting out on the balcony of her earthly apartment. Persephone's work as goddess of spring keeps her up on earth for nine months of the year, so she rents a little place in Athens. I was up for a short visit, relaxing, taking time off from my difficult and demanding duties as ruler of the Underworld. Persephone had on a bright pink robe. She wore a matching headband of pink petunias in her hair. She was chatting on the phone with her goddess girlfriend, Artemis. From what I could tell, they were chatting about the upcoming Olympic games. I was reading the comics in *The Athens Times*. I took a sip of my mocha-necta-java and a bite of my ambro-strudel. (That's a coffee, chocolate, and nectar combo, and coffee cake. Don't try to order this at your local coffee shop. It's for gods only. Nectar and ambrosia are what keep us immortals perpetually young and good-looking.) I flipped to the sports section.

"Oh, no!" I cried as I caught sight of a horrible headline. "Persephone! Listen to this!"

"Hold on a second, Artemis," Persephone said into her little cell phone. She took the phone from her ear. "What happened, Hades?"

"Boar has thrown in the towel!" I said. "He's left the ring!"

"Who lost his ring?" asked Persephone.

I took a deep breath to calm down. "The Calydonian Boar," I said. "He's quit wrestling!"

Persephone frowned. "I thought you rooted for Hawk-Eye."

"Eagle-Eye," I corrected her. "And you're right. I

do. But a wrestler needs worthy opponents. And Boar is the best!"

"That's too bad, Hades," said Persephone. She put the phone back to her ear. "Sorry about that, Artemis," she said. "Now, what were you saying about goddesses' rights?"

I tuned out Persephone and tuned back in to the article. This is what it said.

The Athens Times

WRESTLING IMMORTAL
STEPS OUT OF THE RING

Boar Blames Recent Wrestling Federation Decision

THEBES: Boar, from Calydonia, known as the Calydonian Boar, is one of the greatest wrestlers ever to grace the ring. Now this legend of wrestling has said toodle-oo to the sport. Boar explained what happened. Speaking in his own brand of boarish street poetry, he said:

> "The Flying-Hoof Thrust is my main move,
> Now the Wrestling Federation disapproves,
> They banned my move, they say it's wrong,
> And so to wrestling I say, 'So long!'"

Boar's many fans are weeping and rending their garments over the loss of their champ. Some of them are picketing Wrestle Dome with signs saying "Bring Back Boar!" and "Wrestling Federation: Tusk Tusk!"

His opponents had this to say about Boar's decision to kiss wrestling good-bye.

"Wrestling won't be the same without him," said "Eagle-Eye" Cyclops.

"Yeah," agreed "Squeeze" Python. "It'll be much, much better!"

"Better!" I muttered. "Bah!" Python was just bitter. The Boar had beaten him in IX out of their last X matches. No wonder he was glad to be rid of him! Wrestling was Boar's life. He even ran a wrestling school. I wondered what he'd do now.

"Hades?" said Persephone.

I looked up. "Yes, my sweet?"

"I have to go to work," she said. "I have to go to the hills and fields and make flowers bud, trees leaf, and grass grow."

"All right, my dear," I said. "Have a good day!"

"Hades," said Persephone, "I'd like some help."

I looked up at her, concerned. "Don't you have enough gardening nymphs and sprites?"

"I have plenty of nymphs and sprites," she said. "But I'd like some help from *you*."

"Me?"

"Yes, Hades." Persephone took my hand and pulled me to my feet. "Come on."

As we walked through the apartment, Persephone picked up her gardening basket, gloves, and a couple of bushel baskets. I followed her outside.

"We're astro-traveling to the hills of Arcadia," she told me. "Ready?"

"Uh . . . not really, Phoney, honey," I said. "I was thinking of hanging out on the balcony for a while. Finishing the paper. Relaxing. You know. This *is* my vacation."

"Every day is a vacation for you, Hades," said Persephone. "I mean, really, how hard is it to ride your chariot around the Underworld, checking on things?"

"Huh?"

"My job is huge!" Persephone went on. "Every single flower bud on earth needs me, or it won't open. Every tree needs me, or it won't leaf. I have to go to Brussels and see about every single sprout! Do you know how exhausting that is?"

I frowned. "Artemis put you up to this, didn't she?"

"Artemis didn't put me up to anything," said Persephone. "She just told me about a survey she took. A survey about how much work gods do and how much goddesses do. And you know what, Hades?"

"Let me take a wild guess. Goddesses do more?"

"Exactly. So it's only fair that you help me out a little."

I knew when I was beat. "Let's go."

Together we chanted the ZIP code for the Hills of Arcadia. *ZIP!* We landed on a hillside near a large vegetable garden. I could tell that Persephone had already been there. All sorts of leafy green things were sprouting from the soil.

The truth was, I'd always been curious about Persephone's work. All I knew was that she pointed, said *"Ka-bloom!"* and flowers burst open; leaves popped out. So, even though it wasn't the day I had in mind, I was eager to see how it felt to make bare limbs sprout forth green leaves.

"Here, Hades." Persephone handed me a tool. It had a wooden handle and three brass prongs. It looked something like an eagle's claw.

I pointed the tool at the nearest tree. "*Ka-bloom!*" I shouted.

Nothing happened.

Persephone laughed. "That, Hades, is a weeding tool."

"Weeding?"

Persephone nodded. "It's to help you loosen the soil around a weed's roots so you can pull it out. You can start with the artichoke patch." She handed me a bushel basket. "When you fill this up with weeds, dump it in the woods. I'll be on the other side of the hill, doing some leafing." She waved. "Good luck, Hades!" And she took off.

I watched her go. I thought about astro-traveling back to her balcony and finishing my mocha-necta-java while it was still hot. But then I thought, Oh, why not yank up a few weeds? Persephone would see that I was willing to help her out from time to time. And then things could go back to the way they were.

I carried my weeding tool and my bushel basket over to the artichoke patch. I knelt down and started pulling the leafy green things out of the ground. As I pulled, my thoughts turned to Boar. What a loss to the sport of wrestling! Why had the Wrestling Federation banned the Flying-Hoof Thrust, I wondered? All the Immortals of Wrestling had their special moves. Python had the squeeze. Eagle-Eye was a body-slam guy. Who'd put the kibosh on Boar's move?

It was hot on that hillside. Especially for spring. The sun was beating down. There wasn't any breeze. You mortals are always saying "It was hot as Hades!" But the truth is, earth can get plenty hot and steamy.

Gods work fast, and after about an hour, I'd weeded the entire patch. I stood up and stretched. Hard on the old back, weeding. I wiped the drosis—old Greek-speak for "god sweat"—from my brow as I admired my work. Then I picked up the bushel basket piled high with weeds. I was walking toward the woods with it when I heard a man's voice. Someone was coming! Oh, great! I didn't want anyone—even a mortal—to see me like this, all drosis covered, with dirt under my godly fingernails. I'd left Persephone's apartment so fast I hadn't thought to grab my Helmet of Darkness. If I had, I'd have put it on and—*POOF!*—I'd have vanished! The voice was louder now. Footsteps sounded. I couldn't disappear, so I dumped out the weeds and put the basket over my head. I bent my knees and stooped down at low as I could go. I held still, hoping whoever it was wouldn't notice me.

"It's not your fault you're a girl," said the mortal. Who was he talking to? "No, it isn't. Your daddy is a mean man. Mean as they come."

The mortal hadn't seen me yet. That was good. What was he rattling on about?

"If it was up to me, I wouldn't do this," the mortal said. "Not on your life."

I peeked out between basket slats. Holy Mount Olympus! The mortal was carrying a baby!

I squeezed my eyes shut. Not a baby! Don't get me wrong. I like babies. The only reason Persephone and I don't have any of our own is that the Underworld isn't a great place to raise a family. That, plus Persephone's crazy work schedule. But for some reason, babies seemed to find me. I'd spent years looking after baby Perseus and baby Hercules. That was enough. The last thing I wanted was to end up with another *baby*.

"You're a strong little thing," the mortal said. He was close to me now. "Just hours old, and what a grip you've got on my thumb!"

Surely there was some godly spell I could chant that would change me into a forest mushroom. A grasshopper. A pebble. Anything! But for centuries, I'd depended on my Helmet of Darkness to get me out of scrapes. Any shape-changing spells I'd once known, I'd forgotten.

"Great Mount Olympus!" cried the mortal suddenly. "Who are you?"

I knew he meant me. But I held still as a statue. Maybe he'd go away.

"Show yourself," said the mortal. "Let me spill out my woes to a willing ear!"

I sighed. The jig was up. "I'm listening."

First, Boar. Then, weeding. Now I had to squat here with a basket on my head, hearing the complaints of a sniveling mortal. (You see what I meant about this part of the story being embarrassing?) It was turning out to be a very bad day. But right then, I didn't know how bad.

"I am a servant of the king and queen of Arcadia," the mortal said. He bounced the baby as he spoke. "The queen has just given birth to a daughter."

"But the king was hoping for a boy," I said from beneath my basket. This was the oldest story in the book. At that time, kings were always hoping for sons who could take over their kingdoms someday. As if a daughter couldn't do just as well, or better!

"The king wasn't just hoping," said the servant. "He *ordered* his queen to give him a son."

It was getting hot under that basket. My whole face was damp with drosis. I wished this mortal would tell his tale and be done with it. "Ridiculous!" I said. "Go on."

"The king was so upset when the queen disobeyed him," the mortal went on, "that he banished her from the palace."

Drosis dripped off my eyebrows and onto my cheeks. I wanted to hurry his story along. "And he has no doubt banished the baby, too," I said. "And has ordered you to take her to a cottage in some distant kingdom to be raised by peasants."

"Not exactly," said the servant.

At last I could stand the heat no longer. I whisked the basket from my head and stood up.

"Then what are you to do with the baby?" I asked.

"Give her to the first person I see!" cried the servant. He thrust the baby into my unsuspecting arms, turned, and began running back up the hill.

"I'm not a person!" I cried after him. "I'm a god! You—you can't give me this baby!"

"Just did it!" the servant called over his shoulder. "She's yours now. Her name's Atalanta!"

Chapter II

MAMA BEAR

Was I, King Hades, dread Ruler of the Underworld, some sort of baby magnet?

So it seemed.

Baby Hercules had been big and strong. And when he cried, you could hear it for miles. And baby Perseus? Just ask my dog about him. The very mention of his name sends Cerberus, my three-headed guard dog of the Underworld, diving under the nearest couch.

I looked down at the bundle in my arms and at

the small, peaceful face. Atalanta's eyes were closed. She hadn't made a peep. That was a point in her favor.

Holding her carefully in one arm, I picked up the basket with the other. I tossed some weeds back into it and put baby Atalanta on top. The weeds made a nice soft bed for her to sleep on while I figured out what to do with her.

I set the basket in a shady spot. I sat down next to it. I couldn't take Atalanta back to the palace. Her mother had been banished. And her father was, well, about as kind and loving as my own dad, Cronos. He'd wanted to get rid of me, too. So—you have to give him high marks for creativity—he swallowed me. I spent my whole childhood down in his dark, damp gut. But at least I wasn't alone. I'd had my brother, Poseidon. And my sisters, Hera, Demeter, and Hestia. I looked down at Atalanta. Poor little mortal. She was all alone in the world.

Oh, who was I kidding? She wasn't alone. She had me, Uncle Hades.

"Hades!" It was Persephone calling. She tramped over to me. "Taking a break, Hades?"

"Did you check the garden?" I said. "I pulled out every single weed."

"And every single artichoke plant."

"Oops! Sorry."

"That's all right," Persephone said. "You'll improve with prac—" She stopped. Her eyes widened. "Hades!" she whispered. "In the basket! There's a baby!"

"Say hello to Atalanta," I said, and I told her all that had happened.

Just then Atalanta stirred. She opened her eyes. Big brown eyes. She was a beauty.

"Oh, she's so sweet!" Persephone sat down beside the basket. "Kicked out of the palace for being a girl." She shook her head. "That king should be ashamed of himself!"

"What shall we do with her, Phoney honey?" I asked.

Just then, Atalanta's little mouth turned down. She looked as if she were about to cry.

"Uh-oh," said Persephone.

Atalanta opened her mouth and let out a tremendous wail. Whoa! She would have totally drowned out baby Hercules. What a set of lungs!

Persephone took out her phone and punched in some numbers. "Artemis?" she shouted over the crying. "It's Persephone! Can you come to the Hills of Arcadia? Now, yes. We found a baby. A baby girl!" She flipped the phone closed. "Artemis will know what to do!"

Artemis is goddess of the hunt. A strange goddess for Persephone to call for help with a squalling baby, you're thinking. But Artemis is also the Protectress of Youth and Wild Things. And right then, Atalanta seemed to be both.

ZIP! Artemis appeared before us, courtesy of her astro-traveling powers. She always dressed in animal skins, and that day, she was wearing muskrat. She picked up Atalanta. The crying stopped. "Well, hello, little female," she said. "How did you get here?"

I told Artemis the story of how Atalanta had come to be lying in a basket of weeds. The whole time I talked, the baby stared at Artemis. She seemed fascinated by the goddess's bright yellow hair, which she wore in two long braids.

"Given away, were you?" Artemis said to the

baby. "Males are such nasty brutes. Especially kings. Don't worry, little female. You can join the Daughters of Artemis."

"What's that?" I asked. It sounded like some sort of cult.

"You'd be surprised how many idiot fathers don't want female babies." Artemis shook her head. "So I take care of them until I can find them foster mothers." She tickled Atalanta's chin. "And all you have to do, little daughter, is vow never to marry!"

"She's a little young to take a vow, don't you think?" I asked.

"My daughters don't take the vow until they're older," Artemis said. "You're an exception, Hades," she added, "but most males are so annoying. Who needs them? Here." She held the baby out to Persephone. "Bounce her around a bit. Babies love that. I'll be right back."

Persephone took baby Atalanta, and Artemis ran into the woods. I wondered what she was up to. *The Godly Handbook for Helping Mortals* lays out clear rules about what we gods can and can't do. We bend the rules now and then, but we can't jump in every time mortals get themselves into hot water. If we did, we'd end up doing nothing but saving them from danger, XXIV/VII. Mortals are supposed to call on us by name and ask us to do some very specific task to help them. Then we're allowed to pitch in. But Atalanta was too young to know that.

Persephone walked around, bouncing Atalanta. The baby cooed happily. I had to hand it to Artemis. She seemed to know what babies liked.

"I wonder who she'll get to be Atalanta's foster mother, Hades," Persephone said.

"I hope it's someone without any close neighbors," I said. "That baby can really wail."

We didn't have to wait long to find out. Artemis soon appeared at the edge of the woods with a large brown bear and two cubs.

"This is Honey," said Artemis, nodding to the bear. "She's a wonderful mother."

"For Atalanta?" I said. "You're joking!"

"No," said Artemis. "Honey has fostered several Daughters of Artemis. She's one of the best moms in the forest. And it's a plus that Honey's got cubs now. That's Mojo on the left. The other one's Tiny. They'll be Atalanta's brothers."

Honey gazed at Atalanta. Maybe it was a motherly gaze. But maybe it was a look that said, "What a tasty morsel!" I had to know for sure, so I switched my brain into CCC—short for Creature Communication Channel. Persephone switched in, too. It's how we gods talk to animals.

Hello? Honey? I thought to the bear.

King Hades, the bear thought back. *Queen Persephone. What an honor to meet you.*

She was off to a good start.

Tell me, I thought, *how do you raise little human babies?*

The same way I raise my cubs, Honey thought back. *I feed them well and keep them warm and dry and safe in the cave. My cubs start wrestling right away, and my little Daughters of Artemis always join in. When they're old enough, I teach them to run, climb trees, fish, dig, root for grubs and insects, and pick cherries, nuts, and berries.*

What happens in the winter, when you hibernate, Honey? Persephone thought.

That's only for bears who live in the frozen north, thought Honey.

And how will Mojo and Tiny feel about having a sister? thought Persephone.

They'll love it, Honey thought back. *And don't worry. I won't let them get too rough.*

Honey was passing the child-care quiz with flying colors.

Thanks, Honey, thought Persephone. *Sounds as if you're a fine mom. Hades and I will keep in touch.*

Honey smiled shyly. *Please do. Come by any time. My cave's at the foot of this hill.*

Persephone handed Atalanta to Honey. The Mama Bear nuzzled the baby, making soft purring sounds. Then she tucked her snugly under one arm and grunted to Mojo and Tiny, and the three bears and the baby went into the woods.

I turned to Artemis. "Nice work," I told her.

"Thanks, Hades," she said. "By the way, how did your weeding go?"

"Just great," I told her, hoping that Persephone wouldn't rat on me for my little mistake.

"Well, if you'll excuse me," Artemis said, "I'll get

back to hunting. I had a couple of really angry wild boars cornered when I got your call." She began chanting the astro-traveling spell. *ZIP!* She was gone.

I put my arm around Persephone's shoulder and said, "What a crazy day, huh?"

"Day, Hades?" said Persephone. "It's not even lunchtime yet. I've got a patch of onions, leeks, and garlic that needs weeding. Come on. I'll show you what's what."

And so I spent the rest of that very bad day weeding.

One year later, Persephone and I went to visit Honey for Atalanta's first birthday. We expected to find Atalanta toddling around like any little one-year-old mortal. But when we showed up at the cave, she had on a little fur suit and ran to greet us on all fours, just like Mojo and Tiny.

Hello, Honey, thought Persephone in CCC mode. *Atalanta is a very fast runner!*

Yes, she is, thought Honey. *And how do you like the bear-cub suit?*

So cute! thought Persephone.

Artemis had it made for her, thought Honey. *It keeps her warm and makes her look like a little cub.*

Mojo and Tiny had grown over the year. They were big cubs now. Suddenly, Mojo leaped on Tiny. The two cubs began rolling around on the ground, wrestling. Atalanta didn't wait for an invitation. She dove right into the action, rolling around with her brothers.

She's a natural wrestler! I thought to Honey.

Persephone shot me a look.

Just saying, I told her.

We had such fun celebrating Atalanta's first birthday with the bears. The following year, Persephone and I went back to Honey's cave to celebrate Atalanta's second birthday. Mojo and Tiny were full-grown bears now.

Normally my cubs leave the cave at this age, Honey thought to us. *But Mojo and Tiny are so attached to Atalanta that they're sticking around. The three of them go fishing and grubbing together every day.*

We've brought birthday treats! thought Persephone.

Mojo, Tiny, and Atalanta pressed close.

Persephone opened her bag and passed out caramel popcorn balls. Mojo tossed his into his mouth. He swallowed it whole, then reached out a paw and swiped Atalanta's popcorn ball.

"Grrrrrrrr!" Atalanta growled. She raised one side of her upper lip in a snarl.

Mojo quickly tossed back the popcorn ball.

Persephone and I laughed. Mojo must have weighed CC pounds. But that didn't stop the XXX-pound II-year-old from standing up to him.

You tell him, Atalanta! Honey thought.

Atalanta looked Mojo in the eye and began to eat her popcorn ball very, very slowly. Mojo drooled and looked hopeful. But she didn't give him a crumb.

Atalanta was the boss!

Artemis kept close tabs on Atalanta, too. Each summer, she ran a Daughters of Artemis camp. This way she made sure they all learned human speech and some manners. By the time Atalanta was X years old, she was such an outstanding wrestler that Artemis sent her to a special wrestling camp.

Atalanta loves to wrestle, Honey thought to us the

next time we visited the cave. *She's always pretending that she's wrestling in the Olympics.* She shook her head. *I tell her that the Olympic Games are for gods only. But I guess she can always dream.*

No harm in that, I thought back. I'd wrestled in the very first Olympic Games. Okay, I got pinned by a Titan. But it pleased me that Atalanta was so excited about my old sport.

The next few birthdays when Persephone and I showed up at the cave, Atalanta, Mojo, and Tiny were off somewhere in the woods. It seemed that birthdays didn't mean much to a bear, so we skipped a couple of years.

Actually, more than a couple. Immortals are very bad with time. We have so much of it, really, an endless stream of time. Some of us don't keep track of it the way we should. The next time we went to the cave, Honey had two new cubs. Atalanta, Mojo, and Tiny were nowhere to be seen.

Oh, King Hades, thought Honey. *Queen Persephone. Atalanta isn't here.*

Where is she? Persephone thought back. *Did something happen to her?*

Honey nodded. *Some years ago, Mojo, Tiny, and Atalanta were out fishing. Mojo and Tiny came racing back to the cave. They told me that hunters had captured Atalanta in a net.*

Was she wearing her bear suit? I thought.

Yes, but when she got older, she said all that fur slowed her down, Honey thought. *She used to roll up the bear-suit sleeves. And she chewed the legs off just above the knee.*

So the hunters must have known she wasn't a bear, I thought.

I wish I knew, King Hades, Honey thought back. *Mojo and Tiny looked for her for months. But they never found her.*

You haven't heard from her? Persephone thought.

No, thought Honey as her new little cubs rolled at her feet. *But I haven't heard from Mojo or Tiny either.* She shrugged her furry shoulders. *Bears don't keep in touch. That's just how we are.*

Chapter III

CAN'T BEAR THEM

"I'm not really worried about Atalanta," Persephone told me as we got ready to astro-travel back to Athens.

"I'm not, either," I said. "She's strong and in charge. I'd just like to know where she is."

ZIP! We landed outside Athens.

"I have to run, Hades," Persephone said. "I've got a whole orchard of olive trees without a single olive on any of them. I've got to get over there right away."

"Bye, Phoney, honey," I said, reaching for my phone. "I'll give Artemis a call and see what she knows." I punched in Artemis's number.

"Artemis?" I said. "Hades here. I know. Where does the time go? Listen, Persephone and I have just been to Honey's cave. She told us about Atalanta being captured by hunters."

"Where have you been for the past ten years?" Artemis asked me.

I winced. "Has it been *that* long? Anyway, do you know where she is?"

"Of course," said Artemis. "I'm in close contact with all my Daughters of Artemis. Atalanta lives in the city of Calydon. She likes to hang out at a place called Heroes."

ZIP!

I landed right outside Heroes. It seemed to be some sort of a bar and grill. I walked in. The place had the right name. It was crawling with mortal heroes. I recognized some of them from their heroic pictures in *The Athens Times*. (Sure, there were pictures in the ancient Greek newspapers, taken with a *kamara* [old Greek-speak for "camera"].) Some of the heroes were Argonauts, which meant that they'd sailed on the *Argo* with Jason in quest of the Golden Fleece. (I'd helped out with that quest from time to time, but that's another story.) I spotted Peleus, one of the biggest, strongest Argonauts. He was playing darts with Ancaeus, another Argonaut. Meleager, the prince of Calydonia—the lands ruled by the city of Calydon—as well as an Argonaut, was keeping score. Castor and Polydeuces, two more who had sailed with Jason, were waving empty beer mugs, trying to get the bartender's attention. And was that Hercules heading out the door with Theseus? It was. There were several satyrs, short little goatmen, lounging by the pool table while a centaur—top half human, bottom half horse—tried to sink a shot. Other centaurs looked on. On the far side of the pool table, I spotted three more heroes, Lynceus, Nestor, and Telamon. They sat around a table playing poker with three white-robed young ladies. One had long yellow hair, one long black hair, and the third curly red hair. The three shared a long, brightly colored scarf that looped loosely around each of their necks, then fell down over the redhead's white robe. I looked more closely and saw that it wasn't a scarf, really, but a thick bunch of separate silken threads. Ah, I recognized these ladies now. They were the three Fates: Clotho,

Lachesis, and Atropos. And the silken threads they wore were the destinies of every mortal on earth. It seemed unfair for the Fates to be playing poker. They'd definitely know who had the best hand!

But where was Atalanta?

I stepped up to the bar, happy to see that the menu had some godly refreshments on tap. The bartender brought me a NectaLite. Mmmm. Hit the spot. And then I saw Atalanta. She and Meleager, another Argonaut, were bent over the jukebox, picking tunes. Atalanta had grown into a beautiful young mortal. Her long brown hair fell down her back in waves. She was tall, and as muscle-bound as any of the heroes standing at the bar.

A Greek chorus began singing the original version of "I'm Gonna Live Forever" at the tops of their lungs. This was a big hit with heroes, who liked to think that their great, heroic deeds would be remembered for all eternity.

Atalanta suddenly appeared beside me at the bar. She wore a simple white robe belted with some sort of fur. She was barefoot. "Hades?" she said. "Is it really you?"

"It is," I said. "Artemis told me I might find you here."

Atalanta grinned. "Great spot, isn't it? I discovered it when I got back from my long sea voyage."

"Sit down, Atalanta." I patted a bar stool. "Tell me your tale. How about something to drink?"

"Great." Atalanta plunked herself down next to me. She reached way down the bar and pulled a bowl of peanuts closer. "Blueberry smoothie," she told the bartender. Then she turned to me. "I guess you heard how hunters captured me in the forest."

I nodded.

"I could have taken three of them," she said, popping peanuts into her mouth, shell and all. "Maybe four. But there were ten of them. They tied my hands behind my back. I didn't say a word to them, so they thought I couldn't talk or understand what they were saying. What morons." She tossed down another handful of peanuts. "They took me to a ship's captain. They whispered to him that I was very strong. That I would make an excellent crew member for his ship. They tried to sell me to him for a lot of money. That's when I spoke up.

"'I will crew your ship,' I told the captain. 'But only because I choose to.' And I broke the ropes that bound my wrists." The bartender delivered her smoothie and Atalanta downed it in a single gulp. She wiped her lips on the back of her hand and went on. "The hunters ran away in fear. The ship's captain hired me on the spot. His ship was the *Argo*."

"So you sailed on the *Argo* with Jason to get the Golden Fleece?" I frowned, puzzled. "I helped Jason out quite a few times on that voyage. I never saw you on board."

Atalanta shrugged. "Maybe you didn't recognize me," she said. "I looked pretty much like the other sailors." Once more she reached for the peanuts. At the same time Castor, who was sitting next to her, reached into the bowl and grabbed a handful himself.

"Grrrrrrrrr!" Atalanta growled. She bared her teeth.

"Whoa, sorry, Atalanta." Castor quickly dropped his peanuts. "Didn't know this was your bowl."

Atalanta only stared at him as he withdrew his hand and walked away, looking for another bowl of peanuts.

"I see you haven't given up your bear ways entirely," I said.

Atalanta shook her head, smiling. "Anyway, sailing on the *Argo* was a great adventure. I felt bad about not being able to get in touch with Honey, though."

"She understands," I told her.

"Bears are so cool that way," said Atalanta. "No pressure."

"I'll let her know you're all right," I said. "And Mojo and Tiny, too."

Atalanta smiled. "Tell them I'll come visit as soon as I get back from the boar hunt."

"What boar hunt?" I said.

Atalanta swallowed her mouth full of peanuts and said, "King Oeneus and Queen Althea of Calydonia have called on all the great heroes of Greece to come to this spot."

"So that explains the number of heroes in here tonight," I said. "Another smoothie?"

"Sure," said Atalanta. "Raspberry," she told the bartender. She held out her empty peanut bowl. "Got any acorns?"

He shook his head.

"Peanuts, then." Atalanta gave him the bowl. "See, this huge wild boar used to ravage the countryside around Calydonia. Hunters went after him, but no one could kill him. Then suddenly, the boar disappeared. For years, no one saw him. The farmers grew their crops without worrying that the boar would come and eat them. Everyone was glad to be rid of him. And now," she said, starting in on the peanuts again, "he's back."

"And that's why the king and queen have called all the heroes here?" I asked. "They want you to hunt down the boar?"

Atalanta nodded. Then she chugged her second smoothie.

"Think how proud Artemis would be if I were the one to shoot this boar!" Atalanta's eyes gleamed with delight at the thought of it. She was a perfect Daughter of Artemis: strong, independent, an eager hunter. I saw some of the other heroes glancing at her. She was also very beautiful. I wondered whether she'd already taken a vow never to marry.

"How about another drink, Atalanta?" I said.

Atalanta waved to the bartender. "Cherry smoothie! And another bowl of peanuts, while you're at it." Atalanta sure ate like a bear.

The hero Meleager walked over to where we sat. He had dark curly hair, cut short. He wore a golden loop in his left ear. He smiled at Atalanta. Then he turned to me. "Greetings, immortal," he said, acknowledging my godly glow. "I am Meleager."

"Hades," I said.

"Oh, Lord Hades!" Meleager bowed. "This is a great, great honor."

"Oops!" Atalanta said. "I should have introduced you, shouldn't I? I never remember. We bears just sniff to find out who's who." The cherry smoothie arrived, and disappeared.

"It's Prince Meleager, isn't it?" I said. "Son of the king and queen of Calydonia?"

"This is so," said Meleager. "How did you know, Lord Hades?"

"Oh, we gods know things," I said. "So, are you going on the boar hunt?"

"I'm leading it." Meleager's eyes lit up just as Atalanta's had done.

"It's going to be awesome," said Atalanta. "All the Argonauts together again."

The door to Heroes opened. Meleager glanced up to see who had arrived.

"Oh, no!" he groaned. "It's my mother's brothers. My uncles. I can't bear them!"

"Why?" asked Atalanta. "What's wrong with your uncles?"

"They're troublemakers," said Meleager. "Just wait. You'll see."

The uncles spotted Meleager. They made their way over to the bar. One uncle was short and stocky. He was missing part of one ear. The other uncle was tall and thin. He had a black eye. They looked as if they liked getting into fights. I didn't care to meet these two.

"Excuse me," I mumbled. "Be right back."

I walked over to the side of the room. But I kept my eye on Atalanta. I saw Meleager introduce her to his uncles. Right away, the uncles started giving her a hard time. I slowly made my way back and sat on a bar stool not far from Atalanta so I could listen in.

"Atalanta is coming on the boar hunt, Uncle

Feus," Meleager told the stocky uncle. "She sailed on the *Argo*. She can outhunt most men."

"No way!" said Feus.

"Not a chance!" said the thin uncle.

"She's stronger than you are, Uncle Plexippus," said Meleager.

Plexippus sniffed. "I will never hunt with a woman!"

"Then you'd better stay home." Atalanta stood up. She was a head taller than the tall uncle. "Because I'm going on this boar hunt."

"Oh, yeah?" said Feus. "First you'll have to prove you're up to it by fighting me."

"I won't fight you," said Atalanta. "I don't want to hurt you. But I will prove it by wrestling any hero in Heroes. Pick one."

Feus looked around the room, searching for the biggest, strongest hero of them all.

I looked around, too. At least Hercules had left. Atalanta could never have wrestled him to the ground. No one could. Still, all the heroes in the room were muscle-bound giants.

"I pick Peleus!" said Plexippus. "You have to

wrestle Peleus and pin him to the ground!"

Oh, great! Next to Hercules, Peleus was the mightiest hero of all. He stood out because he shaved his head completely. He was known throughout Greece as a champion athlete.

Atalanta smiled. "Peleus!" she roared from across the room. "Come here!"

The good-natured hero walked over to her. "What is it, Atalanta?"

"Peleus, will you wrestle me?" Atalanta asked.

"Here?" said Peleus. "Now?"

Atalanta nodded. Peleus grinned. And without another word, the two began circling each other. Everyone moved back to give them room. Atalanta sprang at Peleus. She grabbed him around the waist, lifted him up over her head, and began spinning him around and around. She whirled so fast, Peleus became a blur. The next thing I knew Peleus was lying on the floor on his stomach. Atalanta held one arm behind his back. "Say uncle," she said.

"Uhhhhncle," Peleus grunted.

Atalanta let go. "All right!" she cried. "I'm going on a boar hunt!"

Chapter IV

EATS LIKE A BEAR

Peleus slowly stood up. He smiled dizzily at Atalanta. "That was fast," he said.

He didn't seem to have any hard feelings. But Feus and Plexippus looked none too happy about the outcome of the match.

"Nice spin," I told Atalanta. "Is that your best move?"

"I've got lots of best moves." Atalanta grinned. "You think you could fix it so I could wrestle in the Olympic Games?"

"I don't think Zeus would go for mortals competing with the gods," I told her.

"Maybe someday," Atalanta said. "It's always been my dream."

Lots of heroes were leaving the bar now, heading into a back room.

Meleager beckoned me over. "My father has rented the Heroes banquet room for tonight, Lord Hades," he said. "He is throwing a feast for all who will go on the boar hunt tomorrow. It would be an honor if you would join us."

"Oh, do, Hades!" said Atalanta. "Sit next to me. But hurry up. I'm hungry."

"Let me settle up with the bartender," I told her. "I'll be right in."

"Forget it, Hades." Atalanta hooked her arm around my elbow. "I had him put your drinks on my tab."

"You did?"

She nodded. "Had to," she said as we headed into the banquet room. "It's a vow we Daughters of Artemis take: Never let a man pay for your drinks."

"I'm not a man," I reminded her. "I'm a god. God of wealth, as a matter of fact."

"Okay, Hades, you can buy me dinner some time." Atalanta laughed. "Oh, it's so good to see you. I just wish Queen Persephone, Honey, Mojo, and Tiny could be here, too."

I sat down next to Atalanta at a long table. I was glad to see that Feus and Plexippus had been seated way down at the far end. I spied the Fates across the table, a few places down from me. They weren't going on any boar hunt. I figured they must be guests, like me. And the fact that they'd been invited meant there would be immortal food for supper. Whoopie!

Meleager sat across from Atalanta, and next to his mother, Queen Althea. The queen's crown sat crookedly on top of her head of blond curls.

King Oeneus sat beside his queen. He stood now and called out, "Greetings, heroes of Greece!"

The heroes cheered and stomped their feet in response.

"I thank you for coming to hunt the monstrous, fire-breathing boar that is ravaging the fields of Calydonia," the king went on. "Much honor and glory shall be heaped on the head of the hero who slays this mighty beast. I'm also offering a handsome cash reward!"

More loud cheering and stomping from the heroes. The mention of a large cash reward always gets heroes worked up.

"Eat, drink, and be merry!" cried the king. "May the best hero slay the boar!"

The cheering and stomping grew deafening. The one thing heroes truly love is trying to outdo each other to find out which of them is really the best.

Servants appeared. They began pouring glasses of wine for the mortals. And glasses of NectaVino for the immortals.

"I'll have the godly special," I told the waiter when he came by to take my order. He soon reappeared carrying an ambro burger with a side of ambro-fries. Yum!

"Are you worried about your son going off to hunt a fierce wild boar tomorrow?" Atalanta asked Meleager's mother, Queen Althea.

"Oh, my heavens no," said the queen. She turned to Meleager and winked.

"Because I cannot be killed," said Meleager. "Right, Mother?"

That got my attention. Meleager was a very nice young man. But he was, after all, a mortal. And the thing about mortals is, they're mortal. They can be killed. (Sorry to bring it up, but it's the truth.)

"That's right, Meleager," the queen said to her son. "You cannot be killed. Not as long as I have the you-know-what."

"What?" said Atalanta, leaning forward curiously.

"I'll tell you," said Meleager. "When I was a week old, I came down with a terrible fever."

"He was burning up," said his mother. "He was barely alive. I thought I would lose him. Luckily, Lachesis and her sisters were guests at the palace at the time."

"Who's Lachesis?" asked Atalanta. I liked the way she wasn't at all embarrassed to ask when she didn't know something.

"She's one of the Fate sisters," said Meleager. "Clotho is the sister who spins the thread of life for every mortal. Then Lachesis gives each mortal a destiny. And Atropos is the sister with the scissors.

It's her job, when each mortal's time comes to an end, to snip the thread of life."

Atalanta turned to the queen. "So you asked Lachesis if Meleager would live or die?"

"Exactly!" The queen nodded, and her crown wobbled.

"We hear what you're saying, Queen Althea!" Clotho called from where she sat farther down the table. Her yellow hair was so thick and so long that it nearly hid the tiny spinning wheel she held in her lap. Even as she spoke, her hands were busy spinning away.

"I remember that night," said Lachesis, tossing her dark hair. "I told you that as long as the log of holly wood in your fireplace was burning, Meleager would burn with fever."

"That's just what you told the queen." Atropos nodded her head of red curls.

"Then," Lachesis added, "I told you that when the log had burned up completely, Meleager would die."

"That log was burning fast," put in Atropos. "I had my scissors all ready."

"Well, I wasn't about to let that happen," the

queen said. "So I grabbed the poker and raked the log out of the fireplace. Then I called for the servants to bring water. They came and poured water on the holly log. It smoked and steamed, but finally the fire went out. Then I ran to my son in his cradle and his fever was gone!"

"Wow!" said Atalanta. "Just as the Fates said."

"We knew the fever would be gone," said Clotho.

"We totally knew," said Lachesis.

"Even so," added Atropos. "One of these days— snip!"

Some of the heroes began to grumble. I didn't blame them. Heroes like to think they control their own destinies. The Fates knew better than to remind mortals that one day they'd be goners. Especially on the night before a dangerous hunt.

I waved to the waiter. I nodded toward the Fates, pointed to a bottle on the table, and drew my finger across my throat. The waiter nodded. He understood what I meant. No more NectaVino for the Fates.

"You were fated to do that, Hades!" Clotho called to me.

"We knew you would," added Atropos.

Even for a powerful god like me, being around the Fates was unnerving.

"Now I keep the holly-wood log in a chest," the queen was saying. "And I keep the chest hidden in a secret place. I'm the only one who knows where it is."

"I know where it is!" called Lachesis. "So do my sisters!"

"But no one else does," said the queen, her crown teetering now. "And as long as that holly-wood log is safe, my Meleager is safe, too!"

"You are lucky, Meleager," said Atalanta. "You may be very bold on the hunt, knowing you will live."

A pair of centaurs rose from the table. They trotted over to Atalanta.

"Nice mane of hair you've got there," one centaur told her.

Atalanta looked up at him. "Are you talking to me?"

"You bet I am, girlie," said the centaur. "The name's Giddiopeus."

"I'm Trotteus," said the other centaur. "Say, how'd you like to go for a ride?"

I groaned. The waiters should have known better than to serve NectaVino to them. When centaurs have too much to drink, look out!

"No, thanks," said Atalanta.

"Aw, come on," Trotteus insisted. "I can take you on a wild ride!"

A low, rumbling growl rose up in Atalanta's throat. She stared at the centaur, lifting her upper lip slightly.

"Sheesh!" said Giddiopeus. He backed away from the table.

"Really," said Trotteus. "You don't have to get all huffy about it."

Atalanta turned back to me and said, "I wonder what's for dessert."

"You have a hearty appetite, Atalanta," I said.

She smiled. "Bears have the right idea. When there's food around, eat it. Because you never know what tomorrow will bring."

"We know!" Lachesis called from her seat. "We know exactly what tomorrow will bring!"

Atalanta rolled her eyes. "So, Hades," she said, "I hope you're planning to come on the boar hunt."

I shook my head. "I'm not much of a hunter."

"So don't hunt," said Atalanta. "But come and see me bring down the boar!"

I smiled. Atalanta was a true hero. All the heroes I'd ever known were completely sure of themselves. And they loved having an audience for their heroic deeds.

"All right, Atalanta," I said. "I'll come. But you might not see me."

"Oh, so you'll be wearing your Helmet of Darkness?" asked Atalanta.

I almost choked on my NectaVino. "How do you know about my helmet?"

"Oh, we mortals know things." Atalanta laughed. "Anyway, I'll see you tomorrow, Hades. Or . . . maybe I won't."

Chapter V

GRIZZLY TALE

The next morning, I was there when Atalanta, Meleager, and a dozen other heroes met at the edge of the Calydonian Forest. The centaurs, Giddiopeus and Trotteus, gathered with the heroes to come along on the hunt.

"Let's go!" shouted Meleager. He blew a loud blast on a ram's horn and led the way into the forest. Atalanta was right behind him. The centaurs trotted along on either side of her. I kept invisible pace with them. Peleus, Hercules, Theseus, Castor, Polydeuces, and the rest of the heroes followed. Feus and Plexippus brought up the rear.

The heroes carried big iron spears. The centaurs were armed with bows and arrows. Atalanta carried a spear. She had a bow and a quiver of arrows slung over one shoulder, and a dagger tucked into her belt. She was ready for anything. The hunting party strode swiftly through the trees. After a time, the heroes became separated from one another.

Giddiopeus and Trotteus came up to Atalanta, who was now walking off to the side of the other hunters.

"How's it going, gorgeous?" asked Trotteus.

Atalanta just kept walking, her eyes searching the forest for the boar.

The centaurs were slow to take a hint. They trotted closer to Atalanta. Giddiopeus bent down and put his face close to hers.

"How about a good-luck kiss?" he said. He scrunched up his lips.

Atalanta let out a thunderous growl. She sounded like a very angry bear.

"Sheesh!" said Giddiopeus. Then he said,

"Whooooooooa!" because Atalanta had picked him up. She held the huge half-man, half-horse high over her head. Then she bent her knees, leaned back, and heaved him up into the branches of a nearby tree.

Trotteus's eyes grew wide. He whirled around to take off, but Atalanta was too quick for him. She scooped him up and tossed him into the branches of another tree.

"Help!" cried Giddiopeus.

The heroes heard the commotion. They ran to see what was going on.

"Help us down!" called Trotteus.

The heroes stared at the big horse-bodied creatures clinging awkwardly to the tree branches.

Atalanta smiled. "Climb down yourselves!"

"It's not that easy when you've got hooves!" said Giddiopeus.

"And big rear ends!" added Atalanta.

All the heroes cracked up, laughing.

"That's not funny!" said Giddiopeus.

"Neither is being pestered while I'm hunting," said Atalanta. "So long!"

The heroes turned and walked on through the forest, leaving Giddiopeus and Trotteus to get down from the treetops as best they could. They tramped through the woods for hours. I tramped invisibly along with them.

At twilight, with shadows growing long, Polydeuces stopped and cried, "Wild boar in sight!"

Atalanta ran to where he stood. She peered through the trees. I peered, too. There he was. His massive head was bent down as he drank from a pool of water beside a cliff. Even in the fading light, I could tell that this was a huge specimen.

"The boar's back is to the cliff," Meleager said, keeping his voice low. "He's trapped. If we spread out, we can all shoot him at once. Then we shall share the glory. And the cash reward!"

Quietly, the hunters spread out.

Meleager cried, "Greetings, boar! Meet your fate at the hands of the heroes of Greece!"

The wild boar quickly lifted his huge head. I caught a flash of curved white tusk. *Big* curved white tusk. This boar was a giant! He snorted angrily, pawing at the earth.

The heroes drew back their spears. Atalanta fit an arrow to her bow.

The great beast began running at the heroes.

"He's charging!" cried Feus.

"Ready?" said Peleus.

"Aim!" said Meleager.

"Hold it!" said Atalanta.

Plexippus threw down his spear in disgust.

"Aw, man!" cried Feus. "We told you a woman would wreck things!"

"Yeah," agreed a few others. "She's messing up the hunt!"

Atalanta just kept staring at the boar.

I stared at him, too. And I couldn't believe my eyes.

Atalanta was the first to find her voice. "Boar?" she said. "Is that *you*?"

Boar stared back at Atalanta with a pair of beady black eyes. Then he nodded, hanging his head in shame.

"Whoa!" cried Hercules. "Is the boar giving up?"

Peleus groaned. "A boar hunt is *not* supposed to end this way!"

"Right!" called Plexippus. "Let's shoot him now!"

"We can bring him down!" cried Feus.

"No!" growled Atalanta. "This boar isn't a monster. He's my wrestling coach!"

My head was spinning. Sure, this was Calydonia. And the heroes were hunting for a huge, fierce boar. But I'd never thought the boar would turn out to be *the* Boar. The wrestling phenom! Wielder of the Flying-Hoof Thrust! I had wondered what Boar would do after he quit wrestling. Now I had my answer. Ravage the countryside. Lay waste to Calydonia. But why?

Atalanta dropped her weapons and ran to Boar. She put an arm around his bristly shoulder. The two spoke softly to each other, while Plexippus, Feus, and the others grumbled. At last Atalanta turned to face the hunting party.

"It is too dark to travel on," she said. "Let us build a fire. We can sit around it, warming ourselves, while Boar tells us his tale."

"What!" cried Plexippus. "Are we taking orders from a *woman* now?"

"Yeah!" cried Feus. "We give the orders, not her!"

"Right, right!" cried several of the heroes. "We give the orders!"

"So give." Atalanta folded her muscle-bound arms across her chest.

The heroes of Greece looked puzzled. For a long time, no one spoke up.

"Well, it is dark," said Peleus at last.

"And cold," said Castor.

"Not that it bothers *us*," said Hercules.

"Still," said Polydeuces, "we could use a fire."

"And we might as well hear what Boar has to say," said Telamon.

So the heroes went out to gather wood. Soon a heroic fire was raging. Atalanta sat down in front of it. Boar took a place beside her. I sat down invisibly behind him. At last all the heroes gathered around the fire, eating whatever they had brought along for supper.

"Tell us, Boar," said Atalanta, when everyone was settled. "How did you come to this sorry state?"

Boar rose to his hooves. He turned to Meleager and began to speak in his Boarish rhymes:

"Prince man, long ago your daddy, to be nice,
Sent up to Mount Olympus a great big sacrifice.
To every god and goddess he sent up smoke so hot,
But he left out one goddess—one goddess he forgot.
How he could forget Apollo's twin sis?
The fearless huntress, Artemis."

Atalanta drew in a breath. "Go on, Boar," she said. Boar nodded and continued:

"Artemis did rant and rave.
She came to see me in my cave.
She said, 'Boar, the Calydonian king has misbehaved!
Go wreck his fields and wreck his town,
Turn all of Calydonia upside down!'"

"That was you?" exclaimed Meleager. "You were the boar who ravaged Calydonia?" Boar nodded.

"I trampled Calydonian fields and I laid waste,
But that sort of thing isn't really to my taste.
I needed a job—a boar's got to nibble,
So after a while, I went to see the sibyl."

"You went to the Oracle of Delphi?" asked Atalanta. "Was she the one who told you to take up wrestling?" Once again, Boar nodded.

"Sibyl said, 'Boar, get into the ring,
Snort and stomp and do your thing.'
So I went down to Wrestle Dome,
And it became my wrestling home.
All opponents I did bust
With my best move, the Flying-Hoof Thrust.
I roared, I snorted, I stomped and stamped,
And soon I was Immortal Wrestling champ!"

Even though I rooted for Eagle-Eye, I'd always admired Boar. He was a true champion. And what a great show he put on in the ring! I was dying to whip off my helmet and shake his hoof, tell him how much I'd loved watching his matches. But this wasn't the moment. I made myself sit quietly and invisibly where I was.

Boar went on:

"Little wrestlers said, 'Boar, teach us to be cool!'
So I opened up a wrestling school.

They said, 'Boar, teach us to be champs!'
So I opened up a wrestling camp."

"It was a great camp, Boar," said Atalanta. "I
learned so much from you." Boar smiled.

"Little wrestlers came to me,
To get as good as they could be,
I taught them moves and everything,
'Bout how to make it big in the ring."

"But what happened?" asked Meleager. "Why
did you start ravaging again?" Boar stared sadly into
the fire.

"One day the Wrestling Fed up and said,
'Boar, your Flying-Hoof Thrust move is dead.
You can cry—Boo-hoo! Boo-hoo!
But there's nothing you can do.'
Without my Flying-Hoof Thrust,
I could not adjust.
Next match, I got pinned to the mat
In ten seconds flat,

By Python, also known as Snake.
I no longer had what it takes.
My move I couldn't use,
So match after match, I did lose.
Little wrestlers left my school,
They said, 'Boar, you're not so cool.
There's a new spot that's hot—
Python's School of Hard Knots.'
Wrestle Dome said, 'Get out! Get out!
We don't want to see your snout!'
I was hurt, I was mad,
I came back to Calydonia and started acting bad.
I ravaged fields and woods,
Wrecked everything I could!
But I won't do it anymore,
Before you stands one sorry Boar."

It had taken Boar all night to tell his woeful tale. Now the sky glowed pink with the light of dawn. Boar sat down beside the fire. No one said anything for a long time.

"So you'll stop destroying Calydonia?" Meleager said at last.

Boar nodded.

"It's a deal.
I'll stop for real."

Plexippus sprang to his feet. "This is hogwash!" he cried, waving his spear in the air.

"Yes!" cried Feus, jumping up as well. "We came here to kill a boar. I say we kill this one!"

Chapter VI

BEAR HUG

Meleager leaped up from where he sat by the fire. "No, uncles!" he cried. "Your spears will do nothing, for this Boar is immortal!"

"Oh, yeah," said Feus, scratching his stump of an ear. "I forgot." He sat back down.

But Plexippus remained standing. "Maybe Boar is immortal," he said. "But we could have captured him. We could have tied him up and taken him back to the king as our prisoner. Now we have nothing to show for our hunt. And it's all Atalanta's fault!"

Meleager's face turned red with rage. "Stop

picking on Atalanta!" he cried. "She is one of the heroes of Greece!"

"Oooh!" cooed Plexippus. "Is Atalanta your sweetheart?"

"No!" cried Meleager, turning redder still.

"Meleager loves Atalanta!" chanted Feus. "Kiss her, Meleager! Hug her!"

A vicious snarl split the air as Atalanta sprang to her feet. "One hug, coming up!" she cried. She grabbed Plexippus with her right hand. She grabbed Feus with her left. She threw her arms around them, picked them up off the ground, and began to squeeze.

"Uuuuugh!" groaned Plexippus.

Feus just sputtered as her grip grew tighter and tighter.

When Feus and Plexippus were as limp as rag dolls, Atalanta let go. The uncles dropped to the ground, gasping for breath.

"That was a bear hug," said Atalanta. "Want another?"

"No, no!" cried Feus and Plexippus.

"Come on, heroes," said Meleager. "Let us go

back and tell my father that the ravaging is over." He turned to Boar. "You come, too."

"Yes, do," said Atalanta.

But Boar hung his head and said:

"Just one more thing:
I'm ashamed to face the king."

"Don't be," said Meleager. "He's very forgiving."

It warmed my godly heart the way Atalanta and Meleager were helping Boar. Now the former wrestling immortal and the heroes began making their way back to the palace. Plexippus and Feus, still panting and groaning, followed at a distance. I trailed invisibly behind them.

"We'll get Meleager for this," said Plexippus.

"Yeah," said Feus. "We'll make him sorry. Very, very sorry."

I walked invisibly along with the heroes back to Calydonia. I kept an ear out for anything else Plexippus and Fuss might have to say. But they were quiet, stewing about their "bear hug." So I listened in on what Atalanta and Meleager said to Boar.

"You're the only wrestling immortal who used the Flying-Hoof Thrust, Boar," said Atalanta. "So you were the only one hurt when the Wrestling Federation banned it."

Boar nodded.

"I was down all summer,
It was totally a bummer."

"It's more than a bummer," said Meleager. "It's downright suspicious. I'm going to ask my father to look into it. Find out who wanted your move banned."

Boar shook his head.

"Prince man, don't bother
your father.
What's done is done,
I've had my fun."

My godly heart sank when I heard that. Boar was a great wrestler. He was what made the Wrestling Immortals immortal! I wondered—what would it take to lure him back into the ring?

"Hang with me for a while, Boar," said Atalanta.

"I have to figure out what I'm going to do with my life. Maybe we can figure out something together. Maybe you could write down your poems, and I could sell them."

Boar looked skeptical.

"Or, we could open a smoothie bar," said Atalanta. "You own a *brizo*?" (That's old Greek-speak for blender.)

Boar shook his head.

"I know. Maybe if we train really hard, we could wrestle in the Olympic Games!" said Atalanta.

But Boar said,

> *"Atalanta, you were brave,*
> *Thanks for the save.*
> *I think I need some time in my cave."*

With a wave of his hoof, Boar trotted off into the woods.

"Come see me, Boar!" Atalanta called after him. "You can always find me at Heroes!"

Boar had not been gone long when Peleus said, "Shhh! Someone's lurking at the edge of the forest!"

The heroes readied their spears, just in case.

I spied a shadowy figure standing among the trees. I knew it was a mortal, for it had no godly glow. But that's all I could tell.

"Stranger!" called Meleager. "Make yourself known!"

A skinny young man bolted from the trees, his hands in the air, clearly scared to death. He looked small and weak, surrounded, as he was, by muscle-bound heroes.

"Don't slay me, heroes!" the young man cried. "Please! I mean no harm."

"Who are you?" asked Meleager.

"I—I—I'm from *The Calydonian Post*," the young man said. "I'm a reporter."

"A reporter?" cried all the heroes.

"Well, a cub reporter," the mortal admitted. "This is my first assignment."

"I'll give you a quote!" called Peleus.

"I hope you brought your kamara!" said Castor, showing his profile to the young reporter.

"I was first to spot the boar," said Polydeuces.

"It was a big boar," said Hercules. "But not as big as me."

The reporter's hand shook as he tried to get everything down. The booming voices of all the heroes talking at once seemed almost too much for him.

"Quiet!" called Meleager, and the publicity-seeking heroes settled down. He turned to the reporter. "I'll tell you what happened."

The reporter steadied his hand and gave a nod that he was ready.

"There is only one true hero of this boar hunt," said Meleager. "Atalanta."

"No way!" cried Feus.

"We're all heroes!" called out Plexippus.

"Quiet, uncles!" said Meleager. "I organized this boar hunt for my father, and I'll do the talking here. He turned once more to the reporter. He told him all about how Atalanta had recognized her former wrestling coach. The reporter scribbled away.

While Meleager sang Atalanta's praises, I kept my eye on her. She wasn't the blushing type. But I could tell Meleager's praise embarrassed her.

"If Atalanta hadn't stopped us," Meleager finished up, "we would have thrown our spears at Boar. He's immortal. We could never have killed him. We could only have injured him and made him mad. He might have charged and hurt some of us. Atalanta stopped this from happening. Atalanta saved the day."

The Calydonian Post

ATALANTA SAVES THE DAY!

Boar Hunt Turns into Touching Reunion!

CALYDON: Greece has a new hero—a Princess Hero—Atalanta. She sailed on the Argo to get the Golden Fleece. She stalked the boar who was ravaging the fields of Calydonia.

"She's stronger than most men," said Prince Meleager of Calydonia. "And a better hunter, too."

At the hunt, Atalanta recognized the boar they were after as her former wrestling coach, Boar, a once-great Immortal of Wrestling, now fallen on hard times.

"Boar is immortal," Meleager added. He went on to say that if the heroes had thrown their spears at him, they might have made him angry. Then Boar might have charged them, trampling some and goring others with his terrible tusks. He might have left the greatest heroes of Greece lying in a bloody heap while he ravaged the land of Calydonia!

Boar told the hunting heroes his sad tale of woe, which began when the Wrestling Federation banned his best move, the Flying-Hoof Thrust, and ended with him being kicked out of Wrestle Dome for losing so many matches.

The Princess Hero can be found in Calydonia these days, trying to figure out what to do next. Boar has been seen meeting her for a smoothie at Heroes. What the two of them will decide to do is anyone's guess.

OLYMPIC GAMES FOR GODS ONLY

Mortal Told "No Way"

MOUNT OLYMPUS: An unknown mortal has petitioned Zeus to compete in the upcoming Olympic Games. When asked about this, the Ruler of the Universe said, "No way." End of story.

I put down the newspaper. I wondered who the gutsy Olympic-hopeful mortal was. Atalanta? And I had to hand it to that cub reporter. He had written an exciting story. All that stuff about what might have happened if the heroes had hurled their spears at Boar—that was good!

After the boar hunt, I'd come back to Athens. I was sitting on Persephone's little balcony again. She was flipping through seed catalogs. I was chilling with the paper.

"Atalanta is famous now, P-phone," I said.

"Isn't it funny how things work out?" she said.

"Boar hangs out in Calydonia with Atalanta," I murmured. "I wish he'd consider getting back into the ring."

"Why don't you go talk to him, Hades?"

"I think I will." I folded the paper and put it down. "Want to come?"

"It's spring, Hades!" Persephone said. "I don't have a spare moment!"

"Bye, Phoney, honey!" I said, and I quickly astro-traveled to Calydonia—*ZIP!*—before my queenie could think of a garden in some far-flung corner of the earth that needed weeding.

As I zipped away, I pictured Boar stepping back into the ring for his big comeback. I could almost hear the roar of the crowd as his fans welcomed back their champ. I didn't kid myself. Talking Boar into changing his mind wasn't going to be easy. But if any god was up to the challenge, it was I, Hades.

Chapter VII

BEARLY ALIVE!

I landed in front of Heroes. The garden was open. Tender green vines were starting to climb up the garden walls. Daffodils were blooming. Persephone had never mentioned coming to Heroes, but clearly she'd been here. A nice job she'd done, too.

I walked into the garden. All the usual heroes were there—except for Meleager. Was some princely business keeping him from hanging out with his pals? Hercules and Peleus sat at a table facing one another. They had that competitive gleam in their eyes. The other heroes stood in a tight circle around them. They seemed to be egging the two on to do something.

"You can beat him, Hercules!" said Castor.

"You can take him, Peleus!" cried Polydeuces.

"Start, will you?" said Theseus.

With that, Hercules pounded a huge fist on the table. Peleus's fist banged down on the table next to it. There the heroes sat, fist to fist.

Peleus glared at Hercules and chanted: "One, two three, four! I declare thumb war!"

Hercules's and Peleus's heroic thumbs began darting around, each trying to pin the other down in what looked to be a thumb-wrestling tournament. The other heroes cheered and stomped. I had to smile. Being a hero in ancient Greece was a nice gig.

"Hades!" Atalanta spotted me. She broke away from the crowd and came over to the bar where I was standing. She hopped up onto a stool. I saw that she was holding a smoothie glass. Empty, of course.

"Who do you pick to win?" I asked her.

"Hard call," said Atalanta, as the heroes erupted in a cheer. "But Nestor will wrestle the winner of this match, then I wrestle the winner of that match."

She waved at the bartender. "Blackberry smoothie!" She turned back to me. "You just missed Boar."

"Too bad," I said. "What's he up to these days?"

Atalanta shrugged. "Not much. We toss around ideas, but nothing seems quite right to him. He was such a great wrestling coach. I wish he'd take that up again."

A sudden cheer went up from the heroes.

"All right!" Hercules shouted. "I won!"

"Atalanta! Atalanta! Paging Atalanta!" called a voice.

A messenger was walking through the throng of heroes, waving an envelope.

"Over here!" Atalanta called.

The messenger ran over to her. "Wow!" he said. "Are you really Atalanta, the Princess Hero?" When she nodded, he handed her an envelope. Then he held out a little autograph book. "Can I have your autograph?"

"Sure." Atalanta took the book and signed a big letter *A*. "Writing our whole names wasn't big where I come from," she said, handing it back to him.

"Cool! Thanks!" the messenger called as he ran off.

"Get a lot of requests for autographs these days?" I asked Atalanta, as the bartender placed a lavender smoothie in front of her.

She shrugged. "Some. Isn't that weird?" Then she ripped open the envelope. She handed me the sheet of parchment inside. "Do you mind reading it to me?"

I held the parchment and started reading: "'Dearest daughter . . .'"

"What?" cried Atalanta.

"It's from your *father*." I held the letter out to her. "Maybe you should read it."

"No, you," Atalanta said. "It'll go faster that way." And so I read:

"Dearest daughter,
What fun to read about you in The Calydonian Post, *Princess Hero! I always knew you'd amount to something. Please come home to the palace where you belong. We have so much to talk about.*

Your loving father,
The King"

Loving father? This from the dad who had banished Atalanta's mother for giving birth to a girl? This from the father who had handed Atalanta to a servant just minutes after her birth, with orders to give her away to the first person he saw? I glanced at Atalanta. Her mouth was hanging open in surprise.

"You don't have to go," I told her.

Atalanta shook her head, as if to clear it. "My dad banished my mom from the palace. And got rid of me. Still, I've always wondered about him." She drew a breath. "Hades, how about coming with me? I'd really like you to be there when I meet my dad."

I smiled. Atalanta had called on me by name, and asked me to do a very clear-cut task for her. It was almost as if she'd read *The Godly Handbook for Helping Mortals* herself.

"No problem!" I said. "Let's go."

"Great!" Atalanta slid off her bar stool. She ran over to inform the other heroes that she wasn't going to be able to take her place in the thumb-wrestling rotation. She acted as if going to see her father was no big deal. But I knew better. There on the bar was proof that Atalanta was nervous: One blackberry smoothie—untouched.

Atalanta walked beside me through the streets of Calydonia. She was almost as tall as I was, which is tall. Her long legs kept up with my godly stride. Outside Calydonia, we started down the road to Arcadia.

Suddenly, Atalanta stopped. "I heard a groan."

I listened. "Sounds as if someone's hurt."

We hurried down the road. The groaning grew louder. We rounded a curve and there, lying at the side of the road, was a mortal.

Atalanta rushed toward him. "Stranger!" she cried. "We are here to help you!" She knelt down beside the hapless mortal. "Have you been robbed and beaten?" Then she gave a sudden cry. "Hades! It's Meleager!"

I ran to Atalanta. I knelt down beside her as she put her hand to Meleager's forehead.

"He's burning up with fever!" cried Atlanta. "He's barely alive!"

"Fever?" Alarm bells began going off inside my head. "Meleager! Can you speak?"

Meleager only moaned.

"Let's take him home!" Atalanta picked up the prince, and we took off running for the palace.

When we reached it, I banged on the door. A servant opened it and we rushed inside.

"Queen Althea! King Oeneus!" cried Atalanta. "Come quickly!"

Footsteps sounded from down a hallway, and Queen Althea, her crown askew, appeared in the entry hall. When she saw her son, unconscious in Atalanta's arms, she gasped.

"He has a fever," said Atalanta. "A terrible fever. I fear he is close to death."

Queen Althea quickly summoned a servant to take Meleager and put him in his bed. "Put some cold, wet towels on him," she instructed. "Cool him down!"

The servant carried Meleager away. The queen looked helplessly after him. Then she turned back to Atalanta and me. "How is this possible?" she cried. "Meleager will live so long as the log does not burn. The Fates have said so. As long as the log . . . The log!" The queen gasped. She turned and ran from the room. Soon after, we heard a horrible scream. Atalanta and I ran to the queen. We found her on her knees before an empty chest, sobbing.

"The log is gone!" the queen cried. "Gone!"

"Who could have taken it?" asked Atalanta.

"My brothers!" the queen cried. "They must be burning it. If they keep it up, Meleager will die!"

Atalanta sat down beside the queen. "Tell us what happened," she said.

The queen pulled out a hanky and wiped at her tears. "Feus and Plexippus came here after the boar hunt," she began. "Their faces were red. They were gasping for breath."

"Mmm," said Atalanta. Clearly the two had been recovering from her bear hug!

"They told me that at the boar hunt, Meleager had made fun of them," she said, dabbing at her nose with her hanky. "They said he got all the other heroes to call them names, too. Feus the Goose, they said. And Plexippussycat." The queen broke into sobs. "They were so angry and hurt, and I felt so sorry for them. They kept saying I didn't trust them, or I'd tell them where I kept that holly-wood log, and in all the confusion, I must have given the secret away!"

"Queen Althea, where do your brothers live?" asked Atalanta.

"On the far side of Calydonia," she said. "I bought them a house on top of Greek Peak."

Atalanta stood up. "We can do no more for Meleager here," she said. "Come, Hades. We must go and get the log back from Feus and Plexippus— before it is too late!"

Chapter VIII

PAPA BEAR

"It might be better if Feus and Plexippus don't know I'm around," I told Atalanta when we reached the top of Greek Peak and were approaching Meleager's uncles' house. It was a mansion with many columns. I put on my helmet and—*POOF!*—I disappeared.

Atalanta knocked. She banged so hard that the door swung open. Atalanta strode boldly into the house. I stepped invisibly in behind her. And there were Feus and Plexippus, sitting cross-legged in front of the fireplace, toasting marshmallows over the flame from a single log.

"Yikes!" cried Feus when he saw Atalanta.

"How dare you walk into our house without knocking?" said Plexippus.

"I knocked," said Atalanta. "Put that fire out. Now!"

Feus smiled. "Why should we? Our marshmallows aren't even toasted yet."

"Put out the fire to save Meleager from his terrible fever!" cried Atalanta.

"Not a chance," said Plexippus. "We burn the log a little bit each day. We'll make that fever last a long time. And then—"

Together the brothers chanted: "Ashes, ashes, Meleager falls down!"

Atalanta raised her upper lip in a snarl, then thought better of it. "What do you want in exchange for the log?" she asked. "If it is within my power, I shall give it to you."

"Cash!" cried Feus. "And lots of it!"

"Right!" said Plexippus. "Meleager said you were as strong as any man. But let's see how good you are at making money. Bring us a deka-million dollars, or we'll burn the log to ashes."

Atalanta swallowed. A deka-million dollars was a load of cash!

"All right," she said at last. "I will bring you the money. Now, put out the fire. And give me your word you won't light the log again before I come back with the cash."

Feus picked up a vase of flowers. He turned it over and dumped the water—and the flowers—onto the burning log. The small flame went out. "There. Happy now?"

"You have a year," said Plexippus. "If you're not back with the money by then, Meleager's toast!"

"Don't worry, I'll be back," said Atalanta. "And I'll bring you the cash. But can I trust you to keep your word?"

"For that much money, we'll do anything," said Feus.

"Even keep our word," said Plexippus.

Atalanta nodded, turned, and strode out of the mansion. I was right on her heels. When we were partway down Greek Peak, I took off my helmet. *FOOP!*

"Can you believe those creeps?" said Atalanta. "They want a deka-million dollars! Where can I come up with that kind of cash?"

"Don't ask me," I said, hoping she'd take the hint and ask me.

"I won't," said Atalanta. "I know you're the god of wealth, but it wouldn't be right. I have to earn this money myself." We walked in silence for a while. Then she said, "Here are the things I'm good at. Tell me if any of them are worth gigantic sums of money. Okay?"

I nodded.

"Gathering honey?" she said.

"No."

"Climbing trees?"

I shook my head.

"Catching fish?"

"Nope."

"Wrestling?"

"That could work," I said. "But it would take more than a year for you to become a star."

Atalanta thought for a moment. "Running?" she said. "I hate to do it, but I am fast."

"Not a great way to make money. Why don't you like running?"

"Don't ask," said Atalanta.

We came to a road and Atalanta put out her thumb. I put on my helmet. *POOF!* Half a minute later, a wagon screeched to a stop in front of her and gave her a ride. She was a celebrity now, and everyone who saw her was happy to give her a lift. She hitched all the way to Arcadia, and I went invisibly along for the ride.

When we reached her father's palace, Atalanta knocked at the door.

Her father, King Iasus, must have been watching for her, for he flung open the door himself. He had a big belly. A lit cigar stuck out from between his teeth.

"Atalanta!" The king air-kissed her on each cheek, still puffing on the cigar. "The Princess Hero! My heir! So good to have you home again. Come in!"

Atalanta (and I) walked into the palace. The king led her (and me) into a room that looked like an office. He went to his desk and began rummaging around.

"Father," said Atalanta, "in all these years, have you had any word from my mother?"

"Your who?" The king wrinkled his brow. "Oh, her. No, no one's heard from her. She's"—he waved a hand as if waving away a gnat—"gone." He puffed on his cigar, sending a plume of foul-smelling smoke Atalanta's way. He went back to searching his desk. "Ah, here it is." He picked up a stack of parchments. "Atalanta, my famous daughter! Would you mind signing an autograph for me?"

Atalanta looked surprised, but took the quill he offered and wrote her *A*.

Her father flipped to a new sheet of parchment. "One more here." Again, she signed.

"Just one more." Atalanta signed again.

"Good!" The king puffed away on his cigar as he rolled up the parchment and stuck it in his robe pocket. The smoke made me sick to my godly stomach. "Now, let me show you to your room."

"Oh, I'm not staying, Father," said Atalanta. "I only came to see you for myself."

"Don't be silly." Her father threw a hairy arm around her shoulder. "At least take a look at your room," he said, more or less pushing her toward a flight of stairs. "After all the trouble I've gone to, fixing it up."

Atalanta started up the staircase. I was right behind her.

"Take a left at the top of the stairs," said the king, puffing on his cigar. "First doorway on the right. Go on in." I followed Atalanta into a small bare room. It didn't look to me as if her father had gone to any trouble to fix it up. There was a bed in one corner. A small table and two chairs sat next to it. And . . . why were there bars on the window?

Suddenly, *BAM!* The door slammed shut.

Atalanta ran to it. "Hey, what are you doing?"

"Making sure you stay put!" The king grinned through the small barred window in the door.

Poor Atalanta! I could tell her head was spinning. Her father had tricked her. She was definitely having a bad *heir* day.

I wanted to rip that door off of its hinges! I wanted to take Atalanta far, far away from that father of hers. But there's a whole section in *The Godly Handbook for Helping Mortals* about gods interfering between parents and their children. It's a big no-no.

"Now," said the king, puffing smoke into the room. "It's time we found you a husband."

"No!" Atalanta cried. "I am a Daughter of Artemis. I have taken a vow never to marry."

"So what?" said the king. "I have lawyers here who can get me out of any promise I make. Nothing to it. I'll put them on the case."

"No!" cried Atalanta. "I have no wish to marry!"

"Of course you do!" said the king.

A low rumble started in Atalanta's throat. She curled her upper lip in a snarl.

"Oh, cut the wild-animal bit," said the king. "If you don't cooperate with me, I'll send my people to get a certain holly-wood log, and I'll burn it to cinders."

Atalanta gasped. "How do you know about the log?"

Her father answered with another cloud of smoke.

"You are worse than I ever imagined!" she said. "You are a tyrant and a bully!"

"Thank you!" The king smiled around his cigar.

"Now, about that husband. I'm thinking rich prince. Really rich. One who can afford to pay a huge sum to the father of the Princess Hero."

Atalanta was turning red with rage. "Fine," she said. "Find me a prince. I'll marry him, but he'll have to catch me first."

"No conditions!" said her father, spewing smoke. "No ifs, ands, or buts! No prince is going to . . . did you say . . . catch you?"

"Right," said Atalanta.

The king waggled the cigar between his teeth thoughtfully. "A race," he said. "I could put in a running track here at the palace. Build a stadium around it! I've got land enough. Think of the income! All the young princes of Greece could come, week after week, to try to beat you in a race. I could charge entry fees. And admission for spectators. Oh, this could be big! This could be a spectacle!"

Atalanta grew thoughtful. "If I make enough money running the races," she said, half to herself, "I could buy back Meleager's log."

"You get no money!" said the king. "All the money you make comes to me!"

"Who says?" asked Atalanta.

"The contract you signed says so! Right here in paragraph XXV!"

"Contract?" said Atalanta. "I never signed any contract."

"That's what you think," said the king. He pulled the parchments from his pocket and held one up in front of the little barred window. He began to read, "'All cash or money whatsoever earned by Atalanta goes directly to her father, King Iasus.'" Atalanta looked at it. I did, too. It was true. And under all the itty-bitty print, Atalanta had signed her *A*.

The king laughed, still clenching the stub of a cigar between his teeth. "Be careful who you sign autographs for, Princess Hero!"

Chapter IX

TRAPPED!

"I'm here, Atalanta," I said when her father had gone. I took off my helmet. *FOOP!*

Atalanta stared at me, wide-eyed. "This was a trap! I never should have come!"

"How could you have known what your father had in mind?"

"Running races!" Atalanta flopped down on the bed. "I *hate* running. Why did I have to say that thing about catching me first?" she groaned. "If only I could take it back!"

I sat down on the table, hoping it would hold my godly weight. "You said you were a fast runner."

"I am, I am," she said. "I can outrun anyone."

"They why do you hate it?"

"Don't ask," she said glumly.

I'd promised Persephone to help her with some gardening chores, so once Atalanta had calmed down, I took off. But over the next three days, every time I had a spare minute, I put on my helmet and astro-traveled to Atalanta's prison room. Once when I showed up, a photographer was there with the king, taking Atalanta's picture for the newspaper. Another time, I found Atalanta sitting at the table, practicing writing her whole name.

"Dad says that after the races, I'll have to sign autographs so he can charge people for them," she told me. "He's shameless."

Then one morning when I went to see Atalanta, a servant was unlocking her room.

"Your father the king would like you to join him for breakfast," the servant said.

"No thanks," said Atalanta. "I'd lose my appetite."

For a big eater like Atalanta, that was quite a statement.

"Actually, it's an order," said the servant. "Follow me."

Atalanta sighed and followed the servant to the palace dining room. I tagged along.

The king was already seated at the table. He was smoking his cigar and reading *The Arcadia Arrow*. He looked up. "Good morning, daughter! Good news! The running track and stadium are finished!" He grinned and blew some smoke Atalanta's way. "Ah, how I love being king. I can force workers to do their jobs so fast!"

Atalanta sat down at the far end of the table. She just gave him a look.

A servant held out a bread basket and lifted off the cloth. "A mini-muffin, ma'am?"

Atalanta took a teeny muffin from the basket. "A *what*?"

"Mini-muffin," said the servant.

Atalanta held the tiny breakfast treat between her thumb and forefinger for a moment, regarding it, then popped it into her mouth. She didn't even bother to chew. She swallowed, took the bread basket from the servant, and dumped all the mini-muffins onto her plate. She gave him back the empty basket. "Keep 'em coming," she said, and she began popping mini-muffins into her mouth.

"Take a look at this, daughter," said the king. He handed his newspaper to a servant, who brought it to Atalanta. "You're going to be a very busy girl!"

"What!" Atalanta cried when she'd read the headline. "WHAT?"

There was the picture of Atalanta. Here's what the article said:

The Arcadia Arrow

PRINCESS HERO
SEEKS HUSBAND

Atalanta to Race Suitors

ARCADIA: Greece's newest hero, Atalanta, left home at a very early age. Now she's returned to her father's palace and has asked her father to help her find a husband.

"I'm ready to marry now," said Atalanta. "I thought it would be fun to race my suitors. I'll wed the first one who beats me in a race."

Heads up, suitors. Better start doing some serious training. Atalanta can run like the wind. To beat this Princess Hero, you're going to have to be plenty speedy.

The first race will be held at the palace tomorrow. The entry fee for suitors is $XXX. Admission for spectators is $XX. Good luck! And may the best suitor win!

"Father!" Atalanta looked at him in horror. "This is a pack of lies!"

The king looked puzzled. "Of course it is!" he said. "Eat up, daughter. The first race begins in an hour. You don't want to run on a full stomach."

"That," said Atalanta, dumping another basket of mini-muffins onto her plate, "is the least of my worries."

An hour later, I sat down in the gods' section of King Iasus's stadium. (All earthly sports stadiums are required to have at least four god-size seats—just in case immortals decide to pop in.) I was amazed that the king had been able to construct such a large stadium in such a short time. It had an oval of green grass surrounded by a cinder track, and rows and rows of seats. About half of the seats were filled. At the top of the stadium was a box all decked out in purple banners. In it sat King Iasus and an announcer mortal with a large megaphone. Atalanta and V young mortal men milled about by the starting line.

To my right sat Persephone. I'd phoned her, and even though it was spring and she had a million things to do, she had astro-traveled over to the race.

To my left sat Artemis, wearing what looked like mole fur. I'd called her, too. She was steaming. "I'll change that king into a goat!" she muttered. "No, make that a stink bug!"

I nodded. "He deserves it for sure. The Fates are really messing with Atalanta's thread."

"Welcome to the Princess Hero Races!" called the announcer through his megaphone. "The race will be IV laps around the track. Runners, take your marks."

The racers bent down in starting position.

"Get set . . ."

The racers' rear ends lifted. They kept their fingers on the line.

"Go!"

Atalanta and her suitors shot off their marks and started running.

The race was over in a flash. Atalanta ran across the finish line almost a whole lap ahead of the fastest suitor. She was a graceful runner. I wondered why she disliked running so much.

The fans yelled and cheered for Atalanta. She gave them a halfhearted wave and made her way over to the gods' section.

"You showed them, Daughter of Artemis!" cried Artemis. "Keep up the good work and you'll never have to marry!"

Atalanta leaped into the stands and bounded up to where we were sitting.

"Hi, Hades. Hi, Persephone," she said. "Thanks for being here for me. This is so humiliating. Plus, I need to be out making money to save Meleager." She turned to Artemis. "I never said all that stuff in the paper about wanting to find a husband."

"I knew it," said Artemis. "Journalists almost never get the facts straight."

"Especially when the so-called facts are coming from my dad," muttered Atalanta.

At that moment, the king walked onto the track. "Atalanta!" he called. "Some of your fans want autographs. Get down here. Now!"

"Duty calls." Atalanta waved and ran down the stadium steps to where her father stood. We watched as he hurried her over to a table that had been set up in the center of the track. There was a stack of photographs of Atalanta—copies of the one taken of her for the newspaper.

When Persephone and Artemis astro-traveled back to work, I put my helmet on—*POOF!*—and wandered onto the track. I went over to the table where Atalanta was signing autographs. Next to her stood one of her dad's servants. He was collecting V deka-dollars per signature.

A fan stepped up to Atalanta and held out half a dozen photographs. "Okay, sign the first one 'To my good friend Eilieithuyia,'" she said. "And the second one, 'To my good friend Psiticateusias.' And the third one—"

Atalanta's upper lip twitched. I could tell she was

trying to suppress a snarl. At last she growled, "One autograph per customer, and you're gonna have to spell Eilieithuyia."

I smiled invisibly. Maybe Atalanta was a prisoner at the palace, but she was still in charge.

The following week, XXII suitors showed up for the race. And many more spectators. The stands were nearly full.

As before, Atalanta beat her suitors without really breaking a sweat.

Week after week, the races continued. I was always there, but invisible. Artemis always showed up, too. She loved seeing one of her Daughters of Artemis beat the pants off all those mortal men.

Before long, fans had to line up outside the stadium the night before the race if they wanted to get a ticket. It was standing room only. Young mortal men from all over Greece showed up to try to win Atalanta's hand. But week after week, Atalanta outran them all.

Atalanta's father watched every race from his banner-festooned box. He clenched his cigar between his teeth in a permanent grin. He was making a fortune from Atalanta's races. She was doing all the work, but she never saw a deka-dime.

One day after the race, King Iasus came onto the field to congratulate Atalanta. I hovered invisibly behind him to hear what he had to say.

"Nice going, daughter," he said, puffing smoke at her. "I have a surprise for you."

"That this was the last race?" said Atalanta, sounding hopeful. "That you've given up on trying to find me a husband?"

"Actually, I have," said her father.

Atalanta's face lit up. She looked happier than she'd looked in a long time.

"Come!" said her father. "I want to show you the surprise."

I followed them into the palace. The king led the way down a hallway and opened a door to a room filled with barbells, exercise mats, and what passed in ancient Greece for a treadmill.

"Surprise!" the king said. "Your very own gym!"

Atalanta looked puzzled. "Why do I need a gym?"

I was wondering the same thing.

"So you can keep winning!" said the king. "You think I want one of those suitors to beat you and end this gravy train? Fuggetaboutit. I want you in tip-top shape."

Atalanta folded her arms across her chest. "I don't need to work out to beat these guys. I'm not even running my fastest."

"You can go faster?" said her father.

"Don't ask," said Atalanta.

Just then—*POOF!* Artemis showed up. Today she was wearing wolf. "Daughter of Artemis," she said, "I have a surprise for you."

"I hope it's better than the gym," muttered Atalanta.

"Your father has agreed to let you move in with a friend of mine who lives down the hill," Artemis told her. "You'll have your own room and be free to come and go as you please."

"Great!" said Atalanta.

"All you have to do," Artemis went on, "is go to the gym to work out every other day and show up for your race each week."

"What?" cried Atalanta. "Are you on *his* side?"

"I never side with a male," said Artemis. "Especially one as despicable as your father."

"Thank you!" said the king.

"But, Atalanta," Artemis went on, "I want you to continue racing until you have beaten every young man in Greece."

Atalanta groaned.

"Your races are a great victory!" Artemis said. "Every time you run you show the world that females are powerful."

"Oh, great," Atalanta murmured. "Just great."

"Yeah," said the king, smoke billowing from his cigar. "Great!"

Chapter X

THE ROAR OF THE CROWD

I had to duck down to the Underworld for a few weeks. Persephone thinks my job as Ruler of the Universe is a piece of cake. Hah! When I got there, Charon, who ferries the ghosts of the dead across the River Styx to my kingdom, had raised his prices. The ghosts were booing him and throwing things. If I hadn't been there to take charge, things could have gotten ugly.

When I came back to earth, I didn't have to look far to find news about Atalanta. I picked up a copy of *The Arcadia Arrow*, and there it was, right on the front page, above the fold:

The Arcadia Arrow

ATALANTA
WINS AGAIN

Can She Be Beat?

ARCADIA: Experts at the Fast Running Institute have issued a report. They say Atalanta may be unbeatable.

"She is tall and has long legs," said one expert. "She moves fast, too."

"On the other hand," said another expert, "maybe someone out there is faster than she is. We need more money so that we can study this issue further."

Gyms have opened up all over Greece. Suitors are joining them in record numbers. The treadmill business is booming. But so far nothing has helped any of the suitors beat the Princess Hero.

"Come on over to Arcadia and see this phenom for yourself," said Atalanta's father, King Iasus. "Most of the races are sold out," he added. "But we always hold back a few tickets to sell—for the right price!"

I rushed to the palace. Whoa! The races had really taken off. Mortals had pitched tents on the palace grounds so they could be first in line at the ticket window. I decided to remain visible that day. Luckily, there was no line at all at the gods' ticket window.

"Gods' section," I told the ticket seller.

"You're in luck, Lord Hades," he said. "One seat left."

As I climbed up the steps to the godly section, I wondered who was in the other seats. I looked out at the track. There was Atalanta. And I counted IX suitors. So few? What was up with that? Maybe there weren't that many eligible young men left in Greece who thought they had a shot at beating Atalanta.

I climbed higher and spotted Artemis sitting in the aisle seat of the gods' section. No surprise there. But when I saw who was sitting down the row from her, my mouth fell open in surprise. Hera, queen of the Olympians and goddess of marriage. Next to her sat Aphrodite, goddess of love and beauty. What were they doing here?

I started to slide into the empty seat next to Artemis when she jumped up. The fur she was wearing that day looked like opossum. Her jaw was clenched and she looked totally bent out of shape. She and Hera do *not* get along.

"I'm going for some ambro-popcorn," she said. "Want anything, Hades?"

I shook my head. She didn't ask Hera or Aphrodite if they wanted anything before she ran down the steps. I sat down in the empty seat beside Aphrodite.

"Greetings, goddesses," I said. "So have you come to cheer Atalanta?"

"Who is she, *caro mio*?" said Aphrodite, who sprinkled Italian phrases into every conversation.

"The mortal girl." I pointed her out.

"Ah! She is *così bella*! So beautiful—for a big, muscular girl," said Aphrodite. "Why is she down there with all the *uomini*, the young men?"

"You really don't know?"

Both Aphrodite and Hera shook their heads.

"Then why in the world are you here?" I asked.

"Aphrodite and I haven't been getting any bull sacrifices from this region of the earth for a couple of months now," Hera answered.

Only Hera would think to track the earthly locations of her bull sacrifices!

"We came to find out why," Hera went on. "When we got here, we saw that a race was about to begin, so we got tickets." She shrugged. "We didn't know Artemis was going to be here," she added. "You know, Hades, she is the *most* unpleasant goddess. I can't believe she's Apollo's twin. He's so refined and artistic. And she's such a foul-smelling brute."

"*Sì!*" Aphrodite waved a hand in front of her nose. "*Puzza!* She stinks! She needs a spritz of my new *profumo!*"

"So who is this Atalanta, Hades?" said Hera. "And what's with the races?"

I filled Hera and Aphrodite in on Atalanta's story. "Her father, Iasus, is a powerful king, a money-grubber, and a control freak," I finished up. "It's a bad combination."

"Welcome to Princess Hero Race number XVII," called the announcer just as Artemis came back to her seat with her ambro-popcorn. "The race will be IV laps around the track. Runners, take your marks . . . get set . . . go!"

The runners took off.

"Go, Atalanta!" roared Artemis. "Show the world what females can do!"

"Go, suitors!" yelled Hera. "You can beat her!"

"Hera!" I exclaimed. "What are you doing, rooting for the suitors?"

"I'm goddess of marriage, remember?" said Hera. "I *want* one of the guys to win!"

"*Correte, ragazzi!* Run, men!" cried Aphrodite. "Catch the girl! Go! Go! Go! *Via! Via! Via!*"

In spite of the cheering of two powerful goddesses, none of the suitors proved fast enough to beat Atalanta.

When Atalanta ran across the finish line, Artemis jumped to her feet. "Whooo! Whooo!" she cried. "Way to go, Atalanta! Daughters of Artemis rule!"

"*Per favore!*" cried Aphrodite, clapping her hands over her ears. "Please! That hooting will make me go deaf!"

"Oh, *per favore,* yourself!" scoffed Artemis. "You and Hera just can't stand it that Atalanta doesn't need you."

I winced. Why did Artemis have to taunt Hera and Aphrodite? Was she looking for trouble?

But Artemis charged on. "Atalanta has outrun all her suitors," she said. "Soon she'll have outrun every young male in Greece. Then the races will end and Atalanta will never have to fall in love or get m-m-m—whatever."

Hera arched one eyebrow. "Is that right?"

I didn't like the way she said that.

"That's right," replied Artemis.

"Oh, but *cara mia!*" said Aphrodite, with a sly smile. "We can arrange things otherwise!"

Uh-oh. Artemis had done it. These goddesses were going to make trouble for Atalanta. Big trouble!

I trusted that Atalanta would be safe at the room Artemis had found for her, but I made sure to check in when Atalanta went to the gym. And of course I went to her next race. Only VI suitors at that one. The next week, only V young men came to race against Atalanta. The races, it seemed, were nearly at an end.

I thought the following week might be the last, so I made sure to get to the stadium early. I figured there'd be a crowd—possibly even in the gods' section. I made my way to the seats. There was Artemis, wearing what looked like squirrel. Hera and Aphrodite had shown up again, too. Uh-oh. Why were they here?

"Hadino, *tesoro mio!* Hades, darling!" Aphrodite called when she saw me. "We meet again."

I nodded and sat down. I looked out at the

crowded stadium. The place was overflowing. Everyone in Greece wanted to be there to witness Atalanta's last race. I counted IV suitors standing on the track near Atalanta.

"*Solo quattro,*" said Aphrodite. "Only four. And yet . . . one of them may beat Atalanta."

"Not a chance," said Artemis, without looking at Aphrodite. "In fact, after Atalanta wins today, that will be the end of the races."

"Oh, I think not, *cara mia,*" said Aphrodite.

"Don't bet on it," said Hera.

"Why do you say that?" I asked, hoping I could find out what they had up their sleeves.

But Hera only shrugged. "Just a hunch."

In this race, Atalanta crossed the finish line a whole lap ahead of the suitors. Even though it hadn't been much of a race, the crowd roared. They threw flowers down to their Princess Hero.

I ran down to the field to congratulate Atalanta.

"Good going!" I slapped her on the back. "This makes you the fastest mortal in Greece."

Artemis was right behind me. "Way to go, Daughter of Artemis! Now you'll never have to marry."

Atalanta smiled. "The sign-up sheet for next week's race is still blank. If no one signs up by V o'clock tonight, it's over! Maybe by next week at this time, I'll be out in the world, making money to save Meleager."

Artemis and I were telling Atalanta good-bye when a tall mortal young man come over to her. His dark hair was pulled into a long ponytail—a very unusual style for those days. He smiled in a friendly way at Atalanta. He didn't look like an autograph seeker. Artemis took off, but I hovered within hearing distance, pretending to read King Iasus's NO CLIMBING, NO BLOWING HORNS, NO SPITTING, and SMOKE ALL YOU WANT signs tacked to the fence.

"Excellent race, Atalanta," said the mortal.

"Not really," said Atalanta. "All the speedy runners showed up for the early races. These last few races haven't been too exciting."

"That could change," said the mortal. "I'm Melanion, by the way. And I'm signing up for next week's race."

Chapter XI

BEARLY KNOW ME

"Melanion, no!" cried Atalanta. "Don't sign up for the race. Please!"

"Why?" asked Melanion. "Do you find me that unattractive?"

"No," said Atalanta. "I'm just sick of racing."

"One more race won't kill you," Melanion teased her. "Especially since you'll finally have a worthy opponent."

Atalanta eyed Melanion. "You're a fast runner?"

"Very fast," said Melanion.

"Then go be a track star," she said. "Try out for the Olympic Games."

"The Olympics are for the gods," said Melanion.

"For now," said Atalanta. "But, Melanion, I beg you. Find some other way to show off your speed besides racing me."

"No other race offers such a good prize," said Melanion.

Atalanta rolled her eyes. "You just met me. You don't know me. How can you possibly think you want to marry me and spend the rest of your life with me?"

Melanion grinned. "Believe me, I know. Where's the sign-up sheet?"

"If you can't find it, then you don't deserve to race." Atalanta whirled around and began running out of the stadium.

I wondered about Melanion. If he was so speedy, why had he waited so long to come and race Atalanta? I decided to follow him. I ducked behind the bleachers and took my wallet out of my robe pocket. It was a magical wallet, a gift from Persephone. It grew to hold whatever I put inside it, then shrank back down to pocket size. I pulled out my Helmet of Darkness and put it on: *POOF!* I vanished as fast as one of Atalanta's smoothies.

I followed Melanion as he wove through the crowd leaving the stadium. He asked several other mortals where the sign-up sheet was. Just before V o'clock, he found it and signed his name. It was the only name on the sheet.

Melanion left the stadium. He walked past the many tents still pitched on the palace grounds. At last he came to a small tent and went inside.

In the days before they had electricity, mortals went to bed early. They cooked their supper, ate it, and by the time the fire burned down, they were snoring. But after Melanion ate his supper, he kept his fire going. So I kept watching.

It was close to midnight when I spied two cloaked figures hurrying toward Melanion's tent. I couldn't see their faces, but the figures glowed as only gods and goddesses glow.

The two ducked into Melanion's tent.

"We're here, *caro mio*," one of them sang out.

"Let's get down to business," said the other.

What? Was Melanion in cahoots with Hera and Aphrodite?

I snuck invisibly closer to the tent to listen in.

"We've brought the apples," said Hera.

Apples?

I had to get inside that tent. I sucked in my godly gut and squeezed through the flap. It was a tight fit. And Melanion's tent wasn't very big. I had to watch my invisible self or someone would bump into me and I'd be busted.

"I must be nuts, trusting him with my golden apples," said Hera.

Golden apples? What was going on?

"It's for a good cause, Heradina," said Aphrodite.

"All right," said Hera. "Here, mortal, take them." She handed III golden apples to Melanion.

I couldn't believe it! Hera's golden apples were her prized possessions. When Hera married Zeus, our Granny Gaia, also known as Mother Earth, gave Hera a wedding gift of a magical tree that bore golden apples. Hera loved the apples so much that she didn't want to share them. (Not that Hera has ever been big on sharing.) So Hera took the apples to a secret garden and hired a serpent to guard them day and night. And now she was handing over her precious apples to a *mortal*? It didn't make sense!

"Here's the plan, Melanetto," said Aphrodite. "If Atalanta pulls ahead in the race, roll a *mela d'oro*, a golden apple, in her path. She needs *soldi*, money, to help some boyfriend of hers, so she'll go for it *certo*, for sure!"

"Roll it gently," cautioned Hera. "I don't want my golden apples all dented up."

"Atalanta will see the *mela d'oro*," Aphrodite went on. "She will run to pick it up. Then you will pull ahead in the race!"

Melanion nodded. "I get it."

"You have III apples, III chances," said Hera. "Don't fail us!"

"I won't," said Melanion.

Now the goddesses drew their cloaks around their heads and hurried from the tent. I ducked out with them. I heard Hera and Aphrodite chanting the astro-traveling spell to take them back to Mount Olympus. *ZIP!* They were gone. I chanted the spell to get to Persephone's apartment, and away I Zipped, too.

Persephone gasped when I told her about Aphrodite and Hera giving Melanion the golden apples. "I can't believe Hera would do that!"

"You mean cheat in the race?" I asked her.

"No, I mean risk her precious apples," she said. "You have to tell Atalanta about this, Hades. She has to be prepared for what may happen in the race."

"I don't know where Atalanta is," I said. "She's with some mortal friend of Artemis's."

Persephone quickly phoned Artemis. She got the ZIP code for the house where Atalanta was staying, and the three of us went straight there—ZIP, ZIP, ZIP!

"What's wrong?" asked Artemis. Her garment that night was made of black-and-white pelts. It smelled awful. "Has something happened to Atalanta?"

"Not yet," I said. "But Hera and Aphrodite are stirring up trouble." I gave her a fast version of the story.

"I'd like to turn them both into warthogs!" snarled Artemis. "Or maybe just warts!" She led us quickly to a small house in the village and banged on the door.

A mortal woman opened it. When she saw three immortals standing on her doorstep, she nearly fainted.

"Buck up, Clymene," said Artemis brusquely, as she breezed past our hostess into the little house. "Meet Persephone and Hades. Where's Atalanta?"

"She—she's resting," said Clymene, still stunned.

"Wake her up," ordered Artemis. "We have to speak to her."

"Please, sit down, Queen Persephone, Lord Hades," Clymene said, then she hurried off to wake Atalanta.

Moments later, a half-awake Atalanta staggered into the living room. Her hair was disheveled and her eyes not quite open.

"Whassup?" she said.

"Remember that mortal with the ponytail that you met at the stadium today?" I began, and I told her all I knew of Hera and Aphrodite's plan to have Melanion toss the golden apples.

"But why?" asked Atalanta. "Why are they so eager to have me fall in love and marry him? They don't even know me."

"It's not about you," muttered Artemis. "It's about them."

Now Persephone stepped in. "I'm goddess of spring, Atalanta," she said. "I love what I do, and I care about every single tulip bud. If I met some mortal who didn't like flowers? I'd take it as an insult. It's the same for Aphrodite, with love, and Hera, with marriage. When you proclaim that you will never fall in love or get married, it makes them feel bad, as if they haven't carried out their goddess duties very well."

"Weird," said Atalanta. "Anyway, what am I supposed to do about the apples?"

"Just run the race as usual," I told her. "Ignore the apples."

"Yes, Daughter of Artemis," said Artemis. "That way you will win the race. That way you will never have to m-m-m—you know."

Suddenly, Atalanta's eyes lit up. "But what if I picked up the golden apples *and* won the race?"

"Why bother?" I asked. "Why risk losing?"

"For Meleager," said Atalanta. "Don't you see? A golden apple must be worth at least a deka-million dollars."

I saw where this was headed—right into Hera and Aphrodite's hands.

"I can use the golden apples to buy back Meleager's log!" Atalanta was saying. She was wide awake now, and very excited.

"Aren't you forgetting?" I said. "You'll have to hand the apples over to your father."

"No, I won't!" she exclaimed. "The contract my father fooled me into signing says I must give him all the cash and money I earn. But it says nothing about golden apples."

She had a point.

But Artemis looked worried. "Are you sure you can win, Atalanta?" she said. "Because if this Mel-what's-his-face beats you, you'll have to—m-m-m—you know—the M-word!"

"Don't worry, Artemis," said Atalanta. "I won't have to marry."

Hearing the word, Artemis shuddered.

"What if you have to run a long way to pick up a golden apple?" asked Persephone.

"I can beat Melanion," said Atalanta.

"But how?" said Artemis. "How do you know you'll win?"

"Don't ask!" said Atalanta. "Don't ask!"

Artemis, Persephone, Clymene and I sat for hours trying to talk Atalanta out of going after the golden apples. But her mind was made up.

Hera and Aphrodite were going to cheat. But was there some way I could make sure this race was fair to Atalanta? I thought for a while and then broke into a smile. There was a way!

Chapter XII

THE THREE BEARS

The day before the race, I bought a copy of *The Arcadia Arrow*: Here's what it said:

The Arcadia Arrow

ATALANTA'S LAST RACE

Suitor Says He'll Win; Atalanta Says "No Way"

Arcadia: Atalanta's last suitor, Melanion, once held the record at Arcadia's Laurel Leaf Junior High School for the V dekameter dash. But does this make him good enough to beat Atalanta?

"It does," said the confident Melanion. "You can bet money on it."

When asked to comment on Melanion's statement, Atalanta had only this to say: "Don't bet your life's savings."

King Iasus has upped the admission price for this last race. Tickets go on sale first thing tomorrow morning. Word on the street is: get there early! These tickets are going to go fast.

The day of the big race dawned. Persephone and I astro-traveled to Iasus's palace at sunrise. We thought we'd be early enough to score two gods' seats tickets, but we thought wrong. There was only one ticket left.

"Take the ticket and go on up to your seat, Phoney, honey," I said. "I'll wait here until you-know-who shows up. Hey, look! There's Boar!"

"Go say hello, Hades," said Persephone. "I'll go sit down. I want to talk to Artemis about my Olympic event."

She hurried into the stadium, and I ran over to meet the champ.

"Boar!" I called, waving. "Hades, here. Great to see you again."

Boar wrinkled his hairy brow, confused. That's

when I remembered that I'd been invisible the night he told his tale.

"I'm a huge fan," I said. "Does an event like this make you want to return to the ring?"

Boar shrugged.

"I came here to cheer.
Atalanta's gonna win, never fear."

"I hope so, Boar," I told him.

With a wave of his mighty hoof, the former wrestling champ trotted into the stadium.

I looked around and caught sight of III bears.

I quickly switched my brain into CCC mode. *Honey!* I thought, hurrying over to her. She'd dressed up for the race by tying a bright blue scarf around her thick neck.

Lord Hades! thought Honey. *You remember Mojo and Tiny, don't you?*

I took a look at two huge brown bears standing beside her.

You guys have grown, I thought. *Go on in. There may be a scramble for seats.*

Oh, we're okay, Lord Hades, thought Honey.

Atalanta sent us tickets. And she told us what was up with the golden apples. Mojo and Tiny are ready to jump in if she needs help.

Atalanta's bear brothers nodded, and growled their agreement: "Rrrrrrrrrr."

Good, I thought. *See you inside!* The III bears lumbered toward the entrance as I glanced at a nearby sundial. The race was about to begin. I was starting to get nervous. Was my idea going to fizzle?

Hermes's son Pan led a pack of gods and goddesses into the stadium. Pan is from Arcadia, so this was coming home for him. With him were Artemis's twin bother, Apollo, god of light and music; Demeter, goddess of agriculture; and Aphrodite's son, Cupid, the little god of love, with his once-mortal wife, Psyche. And with them was my little brother, Zeus. I wondered what he'd do when he found out the gods' seats were taken.

"Psst, Cupid," I said as he passed me. "Don't even think about zinging Atalanta with one of your love arrows."

"No way," said Cupid. "My mom's all worked up over this race. I'm staying out of it, man."

Someone tapped me on the shoulder. I turned around. "Mom!" I exclaimed. "You came!"

"Of course I did, Hades, my firstborn!" said my mom, the Titan Rhea. She had on her black judge's robe and carried her two bulging shopping bags. "You called, and here I am."

I hurried her into the stadium and up to the banner-strewn box where King Iasus sat.

"King Iasus," Mom said, "I've come to judge this race, make sure it's fair." She wasn't much for small talk. "Put out that cigar. Now!"

The king quickly stubbed out his cigar. He didn't dare argue with a Titan, about smoking or about her judging the race.

"I'll leave you to it, Mom," I said, and I headed for the gods' section. As I climbed, I looked out at the track. The grass was emerald green. Atalanta and Melanion stood near the starting line, stretching. Over to the side, I spotted a god wearing a helmet with little wings on it. Hermes! He stood behind a table with a sign above it that said LAST RACE SOUVENIR STAND. On display were Atalanta T-shirts, Atalanta java mugs, Atalanta chariot bumper stickers that said, THE RACE IS ON! I chuckled. Hermes was god of business, and he always managed to do some.

"Welcome to Atalanta's final race!" boomed the announcer's voice.

Persephone, Hera, Aphrodite, and Zeus were seated in the godly seats. Artemis, wearing fox for the occasion, stood behind them with the other gods. She looked ticked off. Zeus must have kicked her out of her seat!

I sat down on the steps beside the gods' seats. I put up a hand to shield my eyes from the sun and looked around the stadium. A section of seats was filled with mortal females wearing fur headbands. Had to be Daughters of Artemis.

"Today's race will be IV laps around the track," called the announcer. "Runners, take your marks."

Atalanta and Melanion bent down in starting position.

"Get set. . . ." called the announcer.

The runners lifted their rear ends. Melanion's back pocket looked a little bulgy. Was it filled with golden apples? The runners kept their fingers to the starting line.

The stadium grew very still.

"*Buona fortuna,* Melanino*!*" cried Aphrodite. "Good luck!"

"Shhhhhhhhhhhhhhhh!" cried everyone else in the stadium.

When it was quiet again, the announcer said: "Go!"

Atalanta and Melanion shot off their marks.

The crowd yelled, "Go, Atalanta!"

Hera and Aphrodite yelled, "Go, Melanion!"

Atalanta and Melanion were neck and neck rounding the first curve of the track. Neither had pulled ahead. On they raced.

The Daughters of Artemis in the cheering section jumped to their feet. They put their hands in the air. They began doing the wave and chanting, "Daugh-*TER*, daugh-*TER*, daugh-*TER*!"

Now Aphrodite leaped up and cried, "*Andiamo,* Melanino! Let's go!"

Was this some sort of signal?

Yes! Melanion reached into his back pocket and pulled out a golden apple. He quickly rolled it onto the grass in the center of the track.

The crowd yelled, "No fair!" and "Start over!"
The III bears roared in outrage.

Across the stadium, Boar rose up and shouted:

> *"Cheater on the track,*
> *Take that apple back!"*

Zeus's voice thundered out above all the others:
"You go, guy! Whatever it takes to win!"

While all this was going on, Atalanta had darted
to the inside of the track. Without breaking stride,
she bent slightly, scooped up the apple, and stuck it
into her pocket. Then she pivoted and ran back to
the track. She was behind now, and she began to put
on the speed. By the first curve of the second lap, the
two runners were neck and neck again.

"Way to go, Daughter of Artemis!" screamed
Artemis.

Right then, I wished Atalanta were a bear. Or
any sort of creature. Then I could switch into CCC and
send a message into her brain, loud and clear.
As it was, I could only think it: *One golden apple is
enough to save Meleager. If he throws a second apple, let it go!*

But, I wondered, could she?

The runners crossed the starting line again. As they started on their third lap, Atalanta pulled past Melanion.

"Go, go, go, Atalanta!" cried all the Daughters of Artemis.

Atalanta was pulling ahead fast. Melanion reached into his pocket for another apple. This time he tossed it ahead of Atalanta, and it rolled off to the side of the track.

"Leave it, Atalanta!" I called. "Keep running!"

Suddenly a loud voice above me boomed, "Go for the gold, Atalanta! Get me that apple!"

I looked up and saw that King Iasus had grabbed the megaphone from the announcer.

"That's it!" cried King Iasus as Atalanta sprinted after the apple. "Get it! Get it!"

The apple rolled until it hit the wall of the stadium. Atalanta ran for it. She reached the apple, picked it up, and ran back with it to the track. Only then did she shove it into her pocket with the first apple.

Melanion was a quarter lap ahead now. He was

running so fast that his ponytail streamed straight out from the back of his head.

"Catch up, Atalanta!" roared Artemis. "You must win for females everywhere!"

"Forget it, Atalanta!" cried Hera. "You're as good as wed!"

I think it was Hera's jeer that spurred Atalanta to a burst of speed. She ran so fast that her legs were a blur. By the time Melanion started the last lap, Atalanta had caught up with him.

"Fourth and final lap!" called the announcer, who had managed to wrestle his megaphone back from the king.

Everyone in the stadium screamed and cheered.

Once more, Atalanta pulled ahead.

Melanion reached for the third apple. This time he stopped running, drew back his arm and heaved the apple across the track. It bounced once, twice, three times, then rolled under Hermes's Last Race Souvenir Stand and disappeared.

"Ohhhh," Hera moaned. "The dents!"

I jumped up, screaming, "Leave it, Atalanta! Ruuuuuuuuuuun!"

But Atalanta bounded after the golden apple like a dog after a ball. Melanion sped up.

Atalanta raced toward the souvenir stand and dove under it. In an instant, she rolled out from under it with an apple in her hand. She quickly pocketed it and took off for the spot where she'd left the track.

Melanion approached the curve. He was half a lap ahead—and it was the last lap! My godly heart sank. Hera was right, I thought. Atalanta was as good as wed.

Now Honey rose up to her full bearish height and let out the mother of all roars. Suddenly, Atalanta hurled the top part of her body forward and began running on all fours—like a bear!

Atalanta galloped toward Melanion. Her speed was fantastic! She gained on Melanion so fast it looked as if he were standing still. Faster and faster she came, getting closer to her suitor with every bound. Yes! She caught up with him! The two raced, side by side, for the finish line. On they ran, their feet pounding the track.

The suspense was incredible! I was drosissing up a storm.

Now everyone in the stadium jumped up, screaming and shouting and cheering as the two zoomed across the finish line. Everyone erupted in a volcano of cheering.

The race was over!

But ... who had won?

Chapter XIII

BEARING AMBITION

"It's Atalanta by a nose!" called Mom. She had the megaphone now. "Atalanta wins!"

The whole stadium went wild. Boar and the three bears flung themselves into a group hug, roaring and jumping up and down with glee. The stadium shook as if there were an earthquake.

Hera and Aphrodite were screaming, "Rematch! No fair!"

They had a lot of nerve, talking about "fair."

At last mom gave the megaphone back to the announcer. "QUIET!" he yelled.

Everyone settled down.

"Judge Rhea has called the race in Atalanta's favor," the announcer told the crowd. "So if everyone will settle down, Atalanta will run a victory lap."

"No!" cried Atalanta from where she stood on the track. "Let me speak!"

The crowd hushed. Even the immortals. What was she going to say?

"I have raced for months now," Atalanta said. "I have beaten every young man in Greece who came to race me. I'm finished racing. I won't run even one more lap."

"Way to stand up for yourself, Daughter of Artemis!" cried the goddess of the hunt.

"I have a job to do," Atalanta continued. "And now I'm going to do it. I'm going to save my friend, Meleager." With that, she turned and began jogging toward the stadium exit.

"Atalanta!" It was her father. He'd grabbed the megaphone again. "Wait!"

Atalanta stopped. She whirled around and glared up at the King's box, her hands on her hips. "Well?"

"Bring me the apples before you leave," said her father.

"No, bring ME the apples!" cried Hera.

"They're not yours," King Iasus shot back. "My daughter won them, fair and square."

"Ha!" cried Hera. "They're mine, MINE! And they'll always be mine!"

"My lawyers say different!" shouted the king.

"Your lawyers can go jump in the lake!" cried Hera. "It's my tree that bore those apples, and that makes them *mine*!"

While the two argued over the apples, Atalanta simply walked out of the stadium.

"Be right back, P-phone," I said. I put on my helmet—*POOF!*—and astro-traveled to Atalanta's side. *ZIP!* She was heading toward Calydonia. As I fell into invisible step with her, I could hear King Iasus and Hera in the distance, still fighting over the golden apples.

"I'm here, Atalanta," I told her. "But I've got the helmet on. Nice race."

Atalanta smiled. "Thanks. I didn't want to do the bear thing—it *kills* my knuckles." She held up her hand. It was badly scraped up. "But I had to win."

Suddenly, pounding hoof beats sounded behind us. I turned. There was Boar! And hot on his heels were the III bears.

Boar called:

"I'd hold up if I were you.
You need help—here comes your crew."

Atalanta grinned. Then she looked beyond the furry trio and her smile faded.

"Melanion!" Atalanta cried as he came running after them. "Beat it!"

"No!" cried Melanion. "I want to come with you. I want to help!"

"Yeah, right," said Atalanta.

My sentiments exactly.

"I do!" Melanion paused a moment to catch his breath. "Sorry about those apples."

"Don't be," said Atalanta. "They're going to save my friend Meleager. Now, go away."

"First hear my side of the story," said Melanion, walking fast to keep up with Atalanta. "The newspaper didn't get it right. Sure, I held the record for the V-dekameter dash when I was at Laurel Leaf Junior High School, but that was years ago. Now I'm the Laurel Leaf Junior High School track coach."

"So?" said Atalanta.

"So I was camped outside the palace with two of my speediest students," Melanion said. "I coached them and they ran against you." He shrugged. "Just not fast enough."

Atalanta smiled.

"After they lost, they went home," Melanion went on. "I was packing up the tent to go home, too, when twin flashes of white light appeared before me. And suddenly Hera and Aphrodite were standing inside my tent."

"Were you scared?" asked Atalanta, still walking fast.

"Yeah!" said Melanion. "Especially when Hera said I had to help them or I was toast."

"All right," said Atalanta. "You can come with us. But if you try to get these golden apples back, my crew and I will make you sorry."

"I won't!" said Melanion, eyeing Boar's big, pointed tusks. "I'm on your side."

Atalanta and her crew traveled to Calydonia quickly by hitching rides. When Atalanta stood at the side of the road, with her thumb out, the next wagon to come along always picked her up. And by the time the rest of the party stepped out of the bushes, and the wagon driver discovered that he was getting more passengers than he'd bargained for, including invisible me, there wasn't much he could do.

At last we made it to the base of Greek Peak. We walked up to the top, arriving midmorning. Atlanta banged on the door of Feus and Plexippus's mansion.

"What, what, what?" said Feus testily as he opened the door. "Whatever you're selling, we don't want any. Oh, it's you and—" He stopped when he saw Boar and the three bears standing behind Atalanta. He turned and cried, "Plexippus!"

"I've come for the log, Feus," said Atlanta.

Plexippus appeared at the door behind his brother. "Where's the deka-million dollars?"

"I've got better than a deka-million dollars," said Atalanta, and she pulled first one, then a second, and finally a third golden apple from her pocket.

"*Gaaaaaaa*," Feus croaked when he saw the golden apples gleaming in the morning sun.

Plexippus reached out to grab the apples, but Atalanta pulled them away.

"First, the log," she said.

Feus and Plexippus turned and practically tripped over each other in their rush to get the hollywood log. Not half a minute later, they brought its charred remains to the door.

Honey had unwrapped the blue scarf from around her neck. She stepped forward and held it out in her paws. Atlanta nodded, and Feus tossed the log into the scarf. Honey wrapped it up with great care. Atalanta snuffled something to Honey that sounded like thanks. Then she handed over the apples.

"Next stop, the palace of Calydonia!" Atalanta cried. She and her crew headed down the hill.

It would take them a couple of hours to get there, so I figured I had time to astro-travel into

Calydonia and get a bite. *ZIP!* I took off my helmet—*FOOP!*—and went to a little lunch spot called Dino's. I had one of Dino's fine ambro–pot pies and a NectaLite. That pepped me up.

Ah, I felt godly again as I walked out of Dino's. It was good to be visible again, too. Sometimes, when I wear my helmet XXIV/VII, I start to feel as if I'm fading away.

I still had time for a stroll before I went to the palace. I walked down the street and turned a corner, and there were Feus and Plexippus, staring into the window of a jewelry shop. They were talking excitedly, pointing things out to each other. They went into the shop.

As I passed it, I heard them arguing with the jewelry clerk.

"What do you mean you don't accept golden apples?" cried Feus.

"They're gold!" said Plexippus. "G-O-L-D! Doesn't that mean anything to you?"

"Sorry," said the clerk. "Cash or checks only."

I chuckled as I went on past the shop. It hadn't occurred to Feus or Plexippus that golden apples might be hard to spend. Shopkeepers all over Greece knew about Hera's golden apples, and they knew that sooner or later, she always found a way to get them back.

I astro-traveled to the Calydonian palace. *ZIP!* I joined Atalanta and her crew on the doorstep. Atalanta had just finished the introductions.

"Come in, come in," said Queen Althea, her crown for once centered on top of her head. She turned and called, "Meleager! Come, quickly! Atalanta is here, and she's brought back your holly-wood log."

A minute later, Meleager hurried down the hallway. He looked thin and pale, and not very heroic. But he was smiling. "Hey, Atalanta!"

Honey unwrapped the log and Atalanta held it out to Meleager. "You are safe now, Meleager," she said.

"How in the world did you manage to get it?" Meleager looked up at Atalanta. "Thank you. You've saved my life."

"Here, give the log to me," said Queen Althea. "I'll put it back in its secret place."

"Uh, Mom?" said Meleager. "No offense, but I think I'll find a place to hide the log."

"What, you don't trust me with it?" said the queen, her crown sliding sideways.

"I trust you, Mom," said Meleager. "But not your brothers." He hurried back down the hallway to stash the log.

"Let's celebrate!" said Queen Althea. Minutes later, Meleager, Atalanta, Boar, the bears, Melanion, and I were all seated around the royal table. I picked a seat next to Boar.

"So, Boar," I said as a servant passed around a platter of bacon, lettuce, and artichoke sandwiches. BLAs for the mortals, and ambro–BLAs for us immortal types. I'd just eaten, but hey, I've got a godly appetite. I took two. "How is life back at your cave?"

Boar finished the bite he was chewing and said:

> *"Quiet, Lord Hades—*
> *About drives me crazy."*

"So, you miss the action of the ring?" I asked, my godly heart swelling with hope.

Boar nodded.

"I miss it, all right,
All day and all night.
Miss the roar of the crowd,
Miss the cheers, long and loud."

Yessssssssssssssss! This was music to my godly ears.

"Boar, you're a champ and you always will be," I said. "What would you say to me trying to get you back into the ring?"

Boar smiled.

"You get my move back, Hades, my king,
This Boar will roar back into the ring!"

"I'm on it!" I said.

Now I turned to Atalanta, who was sitting on my other side.

"So, Atalanta," I said, finishing off my first sandwich. "Any idea what you'll do now?"

"Yep," said Atalanta as she lunged across the table for another sandwich.

Everyone grew quiet. Everyone wanted to hear what Atalanta, the Princess Hero, was going to do next.

"I've already broken some important barriers," said Atalanta. "When I sailed off with Jason on the *Argo*, I became the first female to go on a major quest."

She sounded like Artemis!

"When I beat all the suitors who came to race me in Arcadia," Atalanta went on, "I earned the title of the fastest runner in Greece. Not the fastest female runner, but the fastest runner, period."

"What now, Atalanta?" said Meleager. "What barrier will you break next?"

"I want to enter the Olympic Games," said Atalanta.

Everyone gasped. I nearly spewed my Necta-Cola all over the tablecloth.

"That's my ambition," said Atalanta. "To be the first mortal to compete against the gods."

Chapter XIV

CAN'T BEAR TO LOOK

The campaign Atalanta waged to be allowed to run in the Olympic Games is worthy of its own book. Let's just say that when every mortal on earth stops sending bull sacrifices, the gods listen.

On the day the games began, the stadium was packed. Every immortal who could astro-travel, walk, run, fly, or slither was there. Plus every mortal with good ticket connections. Artemis had managed to score a front-row seat for her mortal friend Clymene. The mortals were beside themselves with joy at another mortal's being allowed to enter the games. Many of them must have been thinking, "After Atalanta, why not me?" They were stomping and chanting, "Let the games begin!"

At noon, Iris, the rainbow messenger of the gods, carried the Olympic torch into the stadium, and we gods paraded in after her. I was entered in the Wrestling Event. Persephone marched at my side. This was her first Olympics, and she was nervous. She was entered in Weeding—the events were a bit different in those days—and her big competition was her own mother, Demeter. After the gods, Atalanta strode into the stadium. The mortals went crazy, clapping, and cheering.

"Welcome to the Olympic Games!" said Pan, who had a naturally loud voice and didn't need a megaphone. "The first event today will be Weeding."

"Go, P-phone!" I said. "I'll be rooting for you. Get it? *Root*-ing?" I thought maybe a little joke would calm her down.

"Ha-ha, Hades," said Persephone, and she jogged out onto the field.

When the starting cymbal clanged, the weeding began. It quickly became obvious that Demeter didn't stand a chance. Persephone had spent her whole goddess childhood weeding her mom's gardens. Now, all that practice paid off.

After she won, Persephone stood on a platform. Hestia, goddess of the hearth, put a ribbon around her neck. Dangling from it was a gold medal. The official Olympic photographer snapped her picture.

"Congratulations, Phoney, honey!" I said when she came back to the stands. I gave her a godly hug. My queen, a gold-medalist!

The next event was archery. Artemis, looking good in rabbit fur, and Apollo, wearing a plain white robe, ran onto the field with their bows and arrows. They began shooting at twin targets. But each one got bull's-eye after bull's-eye, and finally the crowd got bored and began booing, so the referee declared a tie.

"The next event is the X-dekameter dash," said Pan. "The competitors will be Hermes . . ."

Flapping his helmet wings as well as his sandal wings, Hermes fluttered out onto the field.

". . . And Atalanta!" said Pan.

Atalanta stepped out onto the Olympic track. She'd always dreamed of entering the Olympics as a wrestler. She felt this was her strongest sport. But after all the races at her father's palace, Atalanta was famous for being a runner. When she received a "PLEASE RUN!" petition signed by more than a deka-thousand mortals, she agreed to enter the X-dekameter dash.

When the mortals saw Atalanta, they screamed their little heads off. Clymene cheered louder than anyone.

"Um, Dad?" Pan called to Hermes when the cheering died down. "Lose the wings."

"You're kidding!" cried Hermes. "I'm not taking off my helmet and sandals!"

"Then you will automatically forfeit the race to your opponent," said Pan.

"I should have grounded you more often when I had the chance," muttered Hermes as he ripped off his helmet and sandals. I had to admit, he looked a little naked without them. He called to the gods, "Okay, who wants to loan me some sneakers?"

Cupid ran out with a pair. "Here, man," he said. "Good luck!" He handed them to Hermes, and Hermes quickly put them on.

"Runners, take your marks," said Pan.

Atalanta and Hermes crouched down in the starting position.

It was just like being back at King Iasus's palace. But now the stakes were different. If Atalanta beat Hermes, she'd be the biggest mortal hero the world has ever known. Artemis would be thrilled. And I'd be happy for her. But not all the gods would feel that way. Zeus was so unpredictable. He could easily decide to zap her with a thunderbolt as she ran across the finish line. I started biting my godly fingernails. At least this was a quick dash and not four laps around a track. I couldn't have stood that much suspense.

"Get set. . . ." said Pan.

Atalanta and Hermes stared straight ahead.

Pan yelled, "Go!"

Off the runners raced. They were side by side, running for all they were worth.

Now Atalanta's father's voice rose up above all others: "Go for the gold, Atalanta!" he cried. "Go! Go! Go! Go! Go!"

Neither Atalanta nor Hermes had pulled ahead at the VIII-dekameter marker. Was it going to be a tie? I couldn't bear to look!

Then, at the IX-dekameter marker, Hermes took a funny little hop. He broke stride and Atalanta raced over the finish line a hair ahead of him.

It was pretty much a meltdown in the mortals' section of the stands. Complete strangers were hugging each other and jumping up and down.

Only Pan could have yelled over all the hoopla:

"THE GOLD MEDAL FOR THE X-DEKAMETER DASH GOES TO ATALANTA!"

"No fair!" howled Hermes. "It's these sneakers! They don't fit right. I demand a rematch."

But no one paid any attention to him.

Now Atalanta was happy to run a victory lap. The cheering was so loud, it hurt my godly ears.

After her lap, Atalanta stepped up onto a platform and received her Olympic gold medal.

"Nice race, babe!" called Zeus from the stands. "Come see me after the games. I can help your career!"

Well, I could stop worrying about Zeus zapping Atalanta. The old myth-o-maniac had a crush on her!

As Atalanta posed for her winning photograph, dozens of mortals rushed up to her. They tried to hand her their cards.

Atalanta shook her head, trying to get rid of them, but they kept swarming around. I thought she might need some help, so I ran down to the field.

"We want you to be our spokesperson," a mortal woman was telling Atalanta. "For Breakfast Bites Cereal. Our slogan is 'Eat it on the run!'"

"Never heard of it," said Atalanta, jumping down from the platform.

"Wait!" called the photographer. "I need to take your picture.

"You don't even have to taste it," the woman told Atalanta. "We'll still pay you tons of money to say you love it. This is the *real* reward for winning the gold medal. Will you do it?"

"No!" said Atalanta.

"Yes!" cried her father, the king. He rushed to

her side. "Yes to all endorsements!" He began taking everyone's cards.

"Dad—" began Atalanta.

"Shhhh!" said her father. "I'll handle this."

"Can we finished up here?" Pan called to the crowd still gathered around Atalanta. "The games must go on!"

Atalanta jumped back up onto the winner's platform.

"I'm not selling anything!" she cried.

"Talk to me!" her dad shrieked to the ad mortals. "I'm her manager!"

"No, you're not, Dad," said Atalanta. "You're fired!"

"You can't fire your own father!" said the king.

"I just did," said Atalanta. Then she turned to the mob gathered around her. "Listen to me!" she cried, and they quieted down. "I got to race in the Olympic Games. I won a medal. That's all the reward I need."

"Way to tell it, Atalanta!" cried a fan from the stands.

"After the games are over, my crew and I are taking to the road," Atalanta went on. "We are going to fight for truth and justice. We are going to right wrongs. We are going to make the world a better place."

Wild clapping and cheering followed.

"I'm a hero," said Atalanta. "That's what heroes do. That's all I have to say."

She was about to jump down from the platform again, when the photographer cried, "One picture, Atalanta! One picture!" He aimed his kamara in her direction.

"Okay," said Atalanta. "One of me. And one with my crew."

The photographer took the winner's picture. Then Atalanta waved over her buddies: Meleager, Melanion, Boar, Honey, Mojo, and Tiny. They ran and stood beside her.

"Hey, where's Hades?" said Atalanta, looking around. "He needs to be in this picture, too."

I slid into the group in back of Boar.

"I, II, III," said the photographer. "What do we call Atalanta?"

"A HERO!" we all cried, and he took the picture.

EPILOGUE

Why Zeus left out so many of the good parts in his version of the Atalanta myth is still a puzzle to me. Why he never told how Atalanta started you mortals competing in the Olympics is still a mystery. Maybe Zeus just got up on the wrong side of the bed the day he dictated that one. He does that sometimes. Lots of times, actually. Anyway, now you know the truth about Atalanta's birth, her treacherous father, her kindly foster mama, and her early years as a Princess Hero.

I worked hard, writing this book. When I finally wrote "The End" on the last page of *Go for the Gold, Atalanta!*, I did not send the manuscript straight to my publisher, Hyperion. Nope. I put it in my desk drawer. Thalia, the muse of comedy, once told me that she was a guest speaker at a writing workshop where the teacher advised the students to put their stories away for a while until they "fell out of love with them." I understand that. When you've just finished writing a story, you're sure it's the best thing ever written. But if you don't look at it for a while, by the time you read it again, you can find all sorts of things that you'll want to change and fix up before anybody else takes a look.

After a couple of weeks, I took my story out of the drawer and revised it. Then I asked Hypnos, my first lieutenant, to take the manuscript over to my publisher. Usually, I hear from Hyperion right away. But this time a week passed. II weeks. III weeks. I started to feel anxious. Did he hate my story? Was it so bad he couldn't bring himself to tell me? I lay awake one whole night, imagining the worst. The next morning, I couldn't take it any more, so I went out to my stables, hitched Harley and Davidson to the old chariot, and drove over to Hyperion's office. I'd never been there before, but I knew I was at the right place when I saw a sign that said: HYPERION: CATTLE RANCH AND PUBLISHING COMPANY.

I knocked at the door of Hyperion's large, ranch-style house.

"Hades!" Hyperion exclaimed when he opened the door and saw me standing there. "Boy, howdy! Knock me down with a feather! What are you doing here?"

"I thought I'd come see what a publishing company looks like," I told him. I gazed around the room. There was a big desk piled high with stacks of paper. Other stacks of paper lay all over his chair, all over his couch. They covered the floor. The place was a mess. "So, uh, where is it?"

Hyperion looked a little miffed. "You're lookin' at it, Hades. This is my office. I read manuscripts and edit them. Then I send them out to be printed."

"You mean those are *manuscripts* all over your desk?" I asked.

"Right." Hyperion nodded.

"You mean . . . other gods' manuscripts?"

Hyperion nodded. "Some are written by gods, some by muses, some by mere mortals."

I swallowed. All this time, I'd thought Hyperion was *my* publisher. I had no idea he published other books, too. This was a low blow.

"Well, what did you think of *Go for the Gold, Atalanta!*?" I asked him.

"To tell you the truth, Hades," he said, "I'm sort of swamped right now. I've only had a chance to skim it."

"Oh." Another low blow.

"But I have a couple of questions," he said. "How did Hera get her golden apples back, Hades?"

"After Atalanta beat Melanion in the race, Hera astro-traveled to Calydonia," I said. "She appeared before Feus and Plexippus. They were so scared they tossed her the apples and ran home."

"Dang, that's fine!" said Hyperion. "What about Boar? Did he ever make it back into the ring?"

I fumbled in my pocket and pulled out a newspaper article. I handed it to Hyperion.

The Calydonian Post

BOAR'S BIG COMEBACK

Calydonian Boar Squeezes Python Out of First Place

THEBES: The Wrestling community welcomed back one of its legends tonight at Wrestle Dome. The Calydonian Boar stepped into the ring and soundly trounced his opponent, Python. The cheering for Boar was deafening.

It was an anonymous fan who brought Boar back to wrestling by convincing the Wrestling Federation to remove the ban on his move, the Flying-Hoof Thrust.

When asked to explain why Boar's move had been banned in the first place, former wrestler turned Wrestling Federation President, Knuckles, had this to say: "Python came to us. He said he felt the Flying-Hoof Thrust gave an unfair advantage to hooved wrestlers, and he asked that it be banned. He also offered all us W.F. board members free lessons for our kids at his wrestling academy, Python's School of Hard Knots. What's wrong with that?"

When asked whether Python will be banned from the ring for his bad behavior, President Knuckles added, "Nah, this is wrestling! But we did change Python's wrestling name from 'Squeeze' Python to 'Sneaky Snake' Python. We think he'll do lots better at the box office."

Hyperion read it and smiled. "Dawg! That Python is a sneaky snake. I'm glad Boar made it back into the ring. And what about Atalanta? Did she have more adventures?"

"Tons," I told him. "And right before she went

off on her next adventure, Artemis threw her a party. At the party, she told everyone a big secret she'd been keeping: Clymene was Atalanta's birth mom! Atalanta was very happy to have found her."

"I'll bet," said Hyperion. "So tell me, been doing any thinking about your next book?"

"How about Jason and the golden fleece?" I said. "It's chock-full of heroes and adventures."

"Sounds good," said Hyperion.

"Or I could tell the real story of the Trojan War," I suggested. "Golden apples there, too. Heroes galore. It's long and messy, but the wooden horse is a sure winner."

"Horse stories are always big sellers."

"Or what about me telling the true story of the Odyssey?" I said. "What a journey that was. Lots of monsters. Plus, a witch who turns men into swine."

Hyperion shoved aside some of the papers on his couch and sat down.

"I like 'em all, Hades," he said. "I like 'em all. But tell you what, good buddy. I'm kinda overwhelmed here. I need some time to catch up. How about if I get back to you on this?"

"Sure, sure, whenever," I got up to go and let Hyperion get back to work.

As I rode home to my palace, I felt sort of bummed. What was I going to do with myself, without a book to write? But by the time I reached Villa Pluto, I had a great idea. And it wasn't for my next book.

"Persephone!" I called from my chariot.

She stuck her head out a palace window. "What's up, Hades?"

"Pack your bags, Persephone!" I said. "We're going on our very first vacation!"

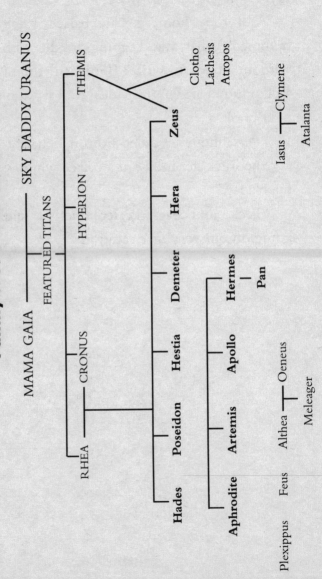

King Hades's
QUICK-AND-EASY
Family Tree of the Gods

MAMA GAIA ———— SKY DADDY URANUS

FEATURED TITANS

RHEA ——— CRONUS ——— HYPERION ——— THEMIS

Clotho
Lachesis
Atropos

Zeus

Hades Poseidon Hestia Demeter Hera

Aphrodite Artemis Apollo Hermes

Pan

Plexippus Feus Althea ——— Oeneus

Meleager

Iasus ——— Clymene

Atalanta

KING HADES'S
QUICK AND EASY
GUIDE TO THE MYTHS

Let's face it, mortals, when you read the Greek myths, you sometimes run into long, unpronounceable names—names like *Plexippus* and *Lachesis*—names so strange that just looking at them can give you a great big headache. Not only that, but sometimes you mortals call us by our Greek names, and other times by our Roman names. It can get pretty confusing. But never fear! I'm here to set you straight with my quick-and-easy guide to who's who and what's what in the myths.

Althea [AL-thee-uh]: queen of Calydonia, mother of the hero Meleager.

ambrosia [am-BRO-zha]: food that we gods must eat to stay young and good-looking for eternity.

Aphrodite [af-ruh-DIE-tee]: goddess of love and beauty. The Romans call her **Venus**.

Apollo [uh-POL-oh]: god of light, music, and poetry; Artemis's twin brother. The Romans couldn't come up with anything better, so they call him **Apollo**, too.

Argonauts [AR-guh-nots]: heroes who sailed with Jason on the *Argo* in search of the Golden Fleece; among the heroes were Ancaeus, Castor, Hercules, Jason, Lynceus, Meleager, Nestor, Peleus, Polydeuces, Telamon, and Theseus.

Artemis [AR-tuh-miss]: goddess of the hunt, the moon, and all young and wild things; Apollo's twin sister. The Romans call her **Diana**.

Atalanta [at-uh-LAN-tuh]: daughter of King Iasus and Queen Clymene of Arcadia; abandoned as a baby, raised by a bear, she gained fame as a great princess hero of Greece.

Athens [ATH-enz]: city of Athena; important city in ancient Greece.

Atropos [AT-ruh-pos]: one of the three Fates, responsible for snipping each mortal's thread when the time comes for that mortal's life to end.

Calydon [KAL-uh-don]: ancient city in western

Greece; capital of Calydonia, which is home to the Calydonian Boar.

Calydonian Boar [kal-uh-DOHN-ee-un]: a monstrous, fire-breathing, wild boar sent as a punishment by Artemis to Calydonia, in northwestern Greece; also said to run a fine wrestling academy.

centaur [SEN-tor]: one of a race of monsters having the head, arms, and trunk of a man and the body and legs of a horse.

Cerberus [CER-buh-rus]: my fine, three-headed pooch, guard dog of the Underworld.

Clotho [KLO-tho]: one of the three Fates; spinner of each mortal's thread of life.

Cupid [KYOO-pid]: The name the Romans gave the little god of love; we Greeks prefer **Eros**.

Cyclops [SIGH-klops]: one of the race of one-eyed giants; among them are Lightninger, Shiner, and Thunderer, children of Gaia and Uranus, and uncles to us gods.

Delphi [DELL-fie]: an oracle in Greece on the southern slope of Mount Parnassus, where a seer or sibyl is said to predict the future.

Demeter [duh-MEE-ter]: my sister, goddess of agriculture and a gardening nut. The Romans call her **Ceres**.

drosis [DROW-sis]: short for **theoexidrosis** [thee-oh-ex-ih-DRO-sis], old Greek-speak for "violent god sweat."

Gaia [GUY-uh]: Mother Earth, the beginning of all life; married to Uranus, Father Sky; gave birth to the Titans, Cyclopes, and the Hundred-Handed Ones; she's my Granny Gaia; don't upset her, unless you're up for an earthquake.

Hades [HEY-deez]: Ruler of the Underworld, Lord of the Dead, King Hades, that's me. I'm also God of Wealth, owner of all the gold, silver, and precious jewels in the earth. The Romans call me Pluto.

Hera [HERE-uh]: my sister, Queen of the Olympians, goddess of marriage. The Romans call her **Juno**. I call her The Boss.

Hermes [HER-meez]: messenger of the gods; also god of business executives, inventors, and thieves; escorts dead mortals down to the

Underworld. The Romans call him **Mercury**.

Hestia [HESS-tea-uh]: my sister, goddess of the hearth; likes to hang around at home. The Romans call her **Vesta**.

Hyperion [hi-PEER-ee-un]: a way cool Titan dude, once in charge of the sun and all the light in the universe. Now retired, he owns a cattle ranch in the Underworld. Has a taste for good books.

Iasus [eye-AH-sus]: evil king of Arcadia; banished his daughter, Atalanta, because he wanted a son.

immortal: a being, such as a god, or possibly a monster, who will never die—like me.

Lachesis [lack-AY-sis]: one of the three Fates; responsible for determining the fate of each mortal.

Melanion [mel-LAN-ee-un]: raced Atalanta; threw golden apples in her path to slow her down so he might win the race.

Meleager [mel-ee-AY-jer]: hero and prince of Calydonia; led the hunt for the Calydonian Boar; the Fates decreed that he would live as long as a certain log made of wood from a holly tree lasted.

mortal: a being who one day must die; I hate to be the one to break this to you, but *you* are a mortal.

Mount Olympus [oh-LIM-pes]: the highest mountain in Greece; its peak is home to all the major gods, except for my brother, Po, and me.

nectar [NECK-ter]: what we gods like to drink; has properties that invigorate us and make us look good and feel godly.

Oeneus [OH-uh-noos]: king of Calydonia, husband of Althea, father of Meleager; called on heroes from all over Greece to go on the Calydonian Boar hunt.

oracle [OR-uh-kul]: a sacred place where a seer or sibyl is said to foretell the future; the sibyl or seer, as well as her prophecy, are sometimes called oracles.

Pan [pan]: son of Hermes; god of woods, fields, and flocks; has a human torso with a goat's legs, hooves, and ears.

Persephone [per-SEF-uh-knee]: goddess of spring

and Queen of the Underworld. The Romans call her **Proserpina**.

Plexippus [PLECK-sih-pus]: brother of Queen Althea of Calydonia and, some say, of Feus; fought with Meleager on the Calydonian Boar Hunt.

Psyche [SIGH-key]: a mortal princess loved by Cupid; her name means "soul."

Python: a huge serpent who guarded the oracle of Delphi; also known as "Squeeze" Python and as "Sneaky Snake" Python; a champion wrestler.

Roman numerals: what the ancients used instead of counting on their fingers.

I	1	XI	11	XXX	30
II	2	XII	12	XL	40
III	3	XIII	13	L	50
IV	4	XIV	14	LX	60
V	5	XV	15	LXX	70
VI	6	XVI	16	LXXX	80
VII	7	XVII	17	XC	90
VIII	8	XVIII	18	C	100
IX	9	XIX	19	D	500
X	10	XX	20	M	1000

satyr [SAY-ter]: a type of woodland god having pointed ears, goat's horns, and goat's legs.

sibyl [SIB-ul]: a mortal woman said to be able to foretell the future; a prophetess.

Thalia [THA-lee-uh]: daughter of Zeus and muse of comedy.

Titan [TIGHT-un]: any of the twelve giant children of Gaia and Uranus.

Underworld: my very own kingdom, where the ghosts of dead mortals come to spend eternity.

Zeus [ZOOS]: rhymes with *goose*, which pretty much says it all; my little brother, a major myth-o-maniac and a cheater, who managed to set himself up as Ruler of the Universe. The Romans call him **Jupiter.**